Dope Girl

*A story of addiction.
A mother's struggle and the
baby girl she left behind.*

Barry,

Thank you so much for the support. I appreciate it greatly. Never be afraid to live your truth!

Be Dope!

Dope Girl

A story of addiction.
A mother's struggle and the
baby girl she left behind.

Written By:
Kimberly D. Mathis

Dope Girl

A story of addiction. A mother's struggle and the baby girl she left behind.

Edition

Library of Congress Catalog - in Publication Data

ISBN 978-0-578-46194-6   KDP-ISBN 9781070641195

Printed in the United States of America

Published by Insight Publishing

References

Scripture taken from the Holy Bible. New International Version. Copyright @ 1973, 1978, 1984 by International Bible Society.

Ed Grabianowski "How Prisons Work" 24 January 2007. HowStuffWorks.com. <https://people.howstuffworks.com/prison.htm> 14 January 2019

Newman, T. (2018, March 2). "What does the liver do?" Medical News Today. Retrieved from https://www.medicalnewstoday.com/articles/305075.php.

Leipholtz, Beth. "The Four Stages of Addiction." 23 December 2016. The Blog. https://www.orlandorecovery.com.

Drug Policy Alliance (January 2018). "The Drug War, Mass Incarceration and Race".https://www.drugpolicy.org.

Acknowledgements

There is so much truth to the societal adage "timing is everything". We all have goals and dreams of doing the things we are great at, the things we are childishly passionate about, the things that bring us great joy or favorable rewards. Then, there are things that we MUST do. It's usually what gives us purpose. It's a task or a movement bigger than ourselves that offers truth, understanding, healing or opportunity. And often, it dominates our minds and burns deep in our souls until it's achieved. It's not always popular or warranted, but certainly necessary. I attempted to write this book twice before over a decade ago, and despite my passion to tell this story for the purposes of my own healing and the healing of those who found themselves in similar situations, the timing just wasn't conducive to where I was in the treacherous process. To put it frankly, not enough time had passed for real, permanent forgiveness and understanding to infiltrate my damaged heart. What I thought was healing was bitterness masked as acceptance. Now, ten years later, "timing is everything" as I am truly healed from the travesty of living with someone else's choices, and the bondage those choices held. I've learned to mend myself on the inside through faith, forgiveness and unyielding self-love.

To my dad, **Ken**, you have been a world class example of love, selflessness and sacrifice. You worked tirelessly to give me opportunities and experiences that would expand my horizons and have great significance on my growth as a person and my future. Thank you for supporting and encouraging me through the years of adolescent stubbornness to adult maturity. For pushing me to reach beyond my limits and for always making me feel like the most important girl in the world. I cherish your consistency and giving heart and all the laughs that we have shared. I am who I am because of you. Thank you for being my hedge of protection, my soft place to fall and my hero.

7

To my husband **Kevin,** you walked into my life at a time when I was broken and angry. I carried the weight of the world on my shoulders. Thank you for loving me in spite of my shortcomings, for always wiping my tears and for encouraging me a thousand times over to step out on faith and let my voice be heard. I am forever indebted to you for walking me off the ledge of fear and for your unwavering support. I love you!

To my children **Kennedy, Kaleb & Kole**, thank you guys for being so patient throughout this process. You inspire me to do more and be better. Kennedy, you were so beneficial in making this book come alive, all of the photo credits belong to you. I appreciate your creativity and attention to detail. Kole, not a day went by that you didn't offer me a hug or a "How's it going mom?" I really admire your caring heart. Kaleb, thank you for being so excited about this project and for burning my ears with continuous "Are you done yet?" and "What's the cover going to look like?", anxiously awaiting the finished product. As you grow older, I hope you guys find strength in this story and are never afraid to live your truth. Let your dopeness shine!

LaTonya Johnson, my sister friend, you've always been more than just a friend, you were like family from the very start. We came into each other's lives at nine years old, clueless about the impact each other would hold. The last 31 years have proven that our friendship and love for each other is timeless and boundless. Thank you for taking on my heartache and pain as your own, for protecting me and for sharing your mom with me. My life just wouldn't have been the same without you by my side. Throughout the process of writing this book, thank you for challenging me to dig deeper, for the impromptu meetings, for answering late night texts, and for your editing and literary sharpness. You've always been one of the smartest people I know. Most of all, thank you for your support and for having my best interest at heart. Kimma and Tonna forever!

Renee Fowler Hornbuckle, I walked into your life 18 years ago as a damsel in distress. Having lacked a relationship with my own mother, you wasted no time embracing me and treating me like one of your own. You continue to show meticulous concern for your role as a mentor and coach. Thank you for being a Godly example and for standing in the gap with prayer. The moment God placed this book in my heart, it was you He told me to call. Without hesitation, you answered and accepted the task with honor. I appreciate you for holding my hand through these unchartered waters and for unselfishly sharing your knowledge and wisdom with me. This book would not have been possible without you. You've helped make my dream come true! I am overjoyed to not only call you pastor but friend. P.S. - next time you bring the coffee!

LaVerne Bell-Tolliver, no amount of words can sufficiently express my gratitude. You knew me before I knew myself and you emotionally protected me before I even could. You are the epitome and my first example of what "my house is your house" truly means. As a child, you welcomed me into your home and always had the perfect words to explain away my inquisitiveness. Thank you for being the world's best godmother, for road trips to Arkansas, for engulfing me in the beauty of African American culture, for vacation bible school, Easter speeches, washed uniforms, game nights, forehead kisses and breakfasts with warm pop tarts. In the very early stages of this book writing endeavor, you told me this book would reach far larger audiences than I had even imagined. Thank you for believing in me and for believing in the healing power of this story.

Hair and Makeup by **Melissa Lewis**. Thank you for your God-given talent. Your magic hands make me look and feel beautiful inside and out! You always challenge me to step outside of my comfort zone and take risks. I appreciate you for that and I marvel at your creativity. Most of all, thank you for your friendship and encouraging and comforting words. Love you Lissy!

9

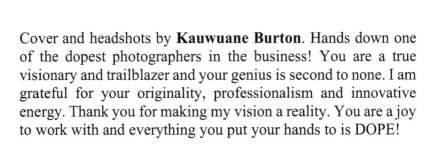

Cover and headshots by **Kauwuane Burton**. Hands down one of the dopest photographers in the business! You are a true visionary and trailblazer and your genius is second to none. I am grateful for your originality, professionalism and innovative energy. Thank you for making my vision a reality. You are a joy to work with and everything you put your hands to is DOPE!

Foreword
Renee Fowler Hornbuckle

There are certain individuals that you meet in life and you instantly know that God put you together. Kim is such a person. When I met her, I knew there was a deep connection…A spiritual association, yet a nurturing connection. A real-life Elisabeth and Mary moment. In the Bible in Luke 1, you see an incredible story of two women who connect and have an incredible bond. I knew that this would be a life-long, purposeful relationship and bond.

At first, I didn't understand why I felt the need to step in as a "proxy" mother to her. As a Pastor and as a Life Coach (or simply as a mature woman), I meet a lot of people who are in need, but this one was unique. I recall with delight sharing with her that I would be honored to be her mother; something that I felt deeply. She was so open to being nurtured, guided, loved and cared for. She had just graduated college and was eager to wed the love of her life: about to become an NFL wife, and enter an amazing world. So feisty, yet tender, correctable and respectful - I claimed she and her family as if they were my own. Every "family" moment was celebrated and appreciated. She was like a little sponge and enthusiastically absorbed my wisdom and accepted my impartation (both positive and corrective). Overtime God began to reveal the reasons why our paths would intersect; I knew exactly what my assignment was with this precious jewel.

You might be asking why someone would be so open to receiving a "proxy" mother. It is in the pages of this book, that frames why God sent me and others like me into her life.

You see when you are born for greatness, regardless of how and where you are born, God has a way of shaping your life, in a way that will benefit you greatly if you are open to receive. It is my belief that God handpicks individuals for your life to serve as your guides, teachers and confidantes. Your guides are important to aid you in maneuvering through life and assisting you in achieving the fullness of your greatness. Perhaps you call them mentors, coaches, friends, and more. The important thing is that you receive who God has sent to keep you and direct you on your path. And in some cases, literally put you on your path to your greatness.

Kim was open. Open to learn, grow and to receive. From the very moment I met her she was searching, but more importantly she was open to receive.

As I watched her be transformed into the beautiful butterfly that she was created to be, and spread her wings, my heart was joyous.

Yet, even in this relationship, the enemy tried to mess that up too (that's another story for another time) … years later, we have found our way, reconciled, reconnected, and we are back to the real purpose of our relationship; our bond.

You will learn throughout the pages of this book, that life happens, but more importantly, it's your response that will determine your outcome. I hope that you will consume each page of this book, reflect on your life and discover that you too can be "dope" in life.

Renee Fowler Hornbuckle
Senior Pastor, Destiny Pointe Christian Center
Arlington, TX

Personal Endorsement
LaVerne Bell-Tolliver, PhD

It is indeed an honor and a privilege to write a personal endorsement for Kimberly Mathis. I have known her almost all of her life, but I had no idea of her talent for writing in such a clear, organized and concise manner until she asked me to read her manuscript. I could not put it down! The content forced me to read about such painful and uncomfortable times in her life that it brought me to tears on several occasions. As her godmother, I thought I knew much about what was happening with her during her young life; however, I realized that was not the case. To this day, I want to comfort her younger self, although she helped me to applaud the fact that she has become a strong, resilient, loving, and determined woman of God.

This book is recommended reading for many types of audiences. Obviously, children, ages ten and older, of parents who abuse substances would gain much insight by reading this book, as would parents who abused substances, legal or illegal, and their partners who are ready to change their lives. As an associate professor emeritus, I continue to present a module to incarcerated males attending a reentry program concerning the effects of their incarceration on their family members.

Kim's book forced me to make a revision in the presentation's content. I previously suggested that children would benefit from having consistent, nurturing contact with their incarcerated parents, provided those parents had not previously harmed their family members and they were legally allowed to maintain relationships with their children.

Kim's narrative helped me see even more clearly the effects of parental substance relapse and subsequent prison recidivism on their children. This book is, therefore, essential reading for

13

helping professionals. It is my honor and privilege to recommend this book to the general public. Readers will have difficulty letting go of the mental pictures and sounds. This book definitely has the potential to change lives!

LaVerne Bell-Tolliver, PhD
Associate Professor Emeritus,
School of Social Work at the University of Arkansas at Little Rock
Pastor, Pleasant Hill Christian Methodist Episcopal Church
Editor of The First Twenty-Five: An Oral History of the
Desegregation of Little Rock's Public Junior High Schools (2017,
The University of Arkansas Press)

Personal Endorsement
LaTonya Johnson

When Kim walks into a room, you're going to see a beautiful petite woman with a glowing half smile, and dimples. She is full of light, very outgoing, and her strength is quiet but strong. Her heart is big. You would never guess her testimony just by looking at her. When Kim asked me to write an endorsement for this book, I must admit, I became nervous and hesitant. After encouraging her for weeks to write her story, fear came over me. Kim said wittingly, "If I can write a whole book, you can write a few pages." That right there is Kim. She has a gift of speaking the truth while encouraging others. She says what she means and means what she says. Kim was absolutely right, if she can unpack all of these words and decades of emotions, surely, I can add some context about my beautiful sister.

Perhaps I am one of the few friends, if not the only one who has met Ms. Rose, and observed the toll the relationship had on Kim throughout the years. I saw the moments of hope which were far and few between jail sentences, and a distant sadness that I couldn't quite reach or protect Kim from. I openly shared my mom with Kim; sometimes feeling jealous of how they talked with ease about certain topics of womanhood including The Talk, but most of the time, I was just happy that me an only child had a sister, or something as close to sisterhood that you can get from two unrelated human beings. We created a blended family before it was even a coined phrase, and it wasn't odd for me to spend time with her father, since my mom was a single parent and my father lived miles away in Wisconsin. Her dad, who I affectionately called by his first and last name, taught us about fine dining and treated us to sporting events; when Kim got an allowance, I got an allowance, too. Perhaps it was the workings of God, but at the young age of nine and ten, we couldn't quite explain it in spiritual terms. It just made sense for our lives, sharing parents, and sharing families.

Ms. Rose, when healthy, was a beautiful, dark skinned woman with high cheekbones and a beautiful smile, as Kim perfectly describes her in this book. But the first time I met Ms. Rose; she wasn't healthy. One Friday after school, as I planned to stay the weekend with Kim and her grandma, we were in the projects at Kim's aunt's house playing outside, waiting for Kim's grandma to get off work and pick us up. Kim and I were racing with other kids in the projects to see who was the fastest. It's just what you did in the projects, race for the title of fastest on the concrete sidewalks. While playing, this woman approached Kim. Even at ten, I was motherly, protective and observant. I wanted to warn Kim, but something in Kim's body language relaxed, softened, and it was apparent that she knew this woman--clothed in mismatch patterns and colors, too big for her tiny frame. She had a scarf on her head, and you can see the hair under the scarf hadn't been touched. She had no visible front teeth. Sadly, at the age of ten, we already knew what this look meant. Even to this very day, it's hard for me to type that Ms. Rose looked like a "crackhead" but that was the term we most often used.

"I'm going to get you something really nice. I'm going to get you something special when I get some money. Ok, baby?"

Kim gave her a half hug, nodding to her words. Then, the lady walked away as randomly as she approached Kim; never knowing where she came from or where she was going. The expression on my face had to be one of judgment but innocent curiosity, as I couldn't make sense of this woman talking to my light-skinned friend. I asked, accenting every syllable with my childhood attitude, "Who-was-that?!"

I just remember Kim's eyes lowering to the ground, as she said, "My mom". In that moment, that was all that needed to be said, as what we had just seen was too intense for two fifth graders on the sidewalk in the projects to put into context. There was no deep psychological conversation that was going to be had.

"I'll race you down the sidewalk," I exclaimed! Trying to break the tension and return us to some sense of childhood normalcy. Nothing ever had to be explained after that moment because it all just made sense. Before that day, I never questioned where Kim's mom was; it wasn't uncommon for our peers to be raised by their grandparents. I don't know what assumptions my ten-year-old mind created to explain why I had never seen or met her mom until that day. I don't know at what point in our growing friendship I would have inquired about her mom. The reality of why Ms. Rose was missing presented itself before I had a chance to ask the hard questions. Maybe in fifth grade, I already knew a missing mom wouldn't have a fairytale ending. Our day in the projects ended with a trip to the corner store with us eating pickles with candy stuffed in the middle. Kimma preferred Sour, I didn't. I preferred Dill, she didn't. She had a dad, I didn't; I had a mom; she didn't. It was just that simple and matter-factly blended.

No matter how hard we tried to be normal, there were painful moments, there were tears, and there was a sense of disconnect in a family where there was dysfunction and other addicts and abusers. There were times, I wish I could just take her away. There were times when I loved how different her family life was from my very small family. They were colorful. There were good times, too: dancing and entering talent shows, exchanging clothes and jewelry, sitting on the stoop of the projects just hanging out like we were in a safe space; and of course, the attention from boys. Looking back, all of those moments were haunted by something dark lurking in the background that our young minds filtered out to cope. I've jokingly said many times, instead of lions, tigers, and bears, we had to navigate through predators, junkies, and dealers.

When reading this book one of the first things you will learn is that Kim loves details. Whereas I was a macro girl who saw the big picture, Kim was the one who made sure everything was perfect. Growing up, our ponytails were slicked to perfection, our uniforms ironed and creased, and our hair bows coordinated with our outfits.

This is the reason why I didn't fully realize the true amount of hurt Kim was carrying, and why many people when they first meet her, wouldn't ever know what she was dealing with at home.

I believe this is one of the most valuable lessons that she received from her grandma; it started in the details of something as simple as making up the bed. There were rules. You did not sit on the bed after it was made and the very first thing you did in the morning at Kim's house was make your bed. Fitted sheets pulled tightly, every single wrinkle smoothed out by hand, the top sheet creased and tucked precisely on the bottom corners, folded over at the top and then tucked neatly on the sides; wrinkle free. The bedspread was placed perfectly symmetrical, folded as well and tucked into the bottom corners. Then there were pillows upon pillows each carefully laid, and a teddy bear or a few stuffed animals carefully placed to finish. We didn't fight much, but if I didn't make up the bed the correct way, Kim would literally take the covers off and re-do it from start to finish, just as precise as her Grandma taught her. All of my hard work was undone over the slightest error. I would get so frustrated, but as an adult, I get it. It's truly a gift! She loved it when everything was beautiful, and presentation was something she had mastered early.

Despite many of the hardships that came from a dysfunctional family, that's the one beautiful lesson she carries with her to this day. Perfecting details and making everyone and everything around her more beautiful, including the memory of her mom whose life was layered with complications. That is the theme throughout her life, beauty!

I hope by writing this book and revealing her truth that she can let go of so many things in the past that she kept hidden, even from me. Those times when her eyes were glossy from a tear that never fell, or those times when her dimples hid the hurt.

Some people will read this and miss the beauty in it; the way Kim honors her mother in a world and family that did not, even in her death. We are taught not to talk about these things because they're private, but they stay inside and eat away at us no matter how beautiful things appear. People including loved ones can deal better with reality when we don't suffer in silence.

What Kim does with this book is beautiful to her soul. It's not a tragic tale, the beauty is the miracle of the life of Kim. Plus, the dignity of the legacy of Ms. Rose, in a world that now understands addiction better.

LaTonya Johnson
Sister Friend since 5th Grade

About the Author

Kimberly D. Mathis is a native of Dallas, Texas and a 1996 honors graduate of Skyline High School. After graduation, she went on to attend Texas A&M University-Commerce on a full academic scholarship awarded through the prestigious Roger Alsabrook Foundation. At Texas A&M-Commerce, she was a frequent affiliate of the Dean's List and a member of the Lions co-ed cheer squad. In 1998 she became a proud member of the prominent Alpha Kappa Alpha Sorority, Incorporated and earned 3rd place honors for Outstanding Undergraduate Chapter President in the South-Central Region. Kim graduated with a Bachelor of Business Administration in the Spring of 2000. Immediately following, she entered the workforce as a Research Analyst for Electronic Data Systems (EDS) in Plano, Texas and served as assistant marketing director for the COMDEX Convention in Las Vegas, Nevada in 2001. Pulling on her corporate experience and business education, she became a member of the Women of Influence, Incorporated Conference Executive Board and Sponsorship Committee Chairman.

Later in 2003, she would launch her entrepreneurial passions and become a franchisee co-owner of Wings-To-Go. In 2006 she earned a Texas Realtors License before taking a position as an income tax professional at Income Tax Specialists in Dallas, Texas. Kim has been a registered preparer with the Internal Revenue Service since 2006 and currently owns and operates her own income tax service, The Tax Lady. She also serves as Vice President of the Kevin Mathis Foundation, a nonprofit charity founded in 2004 that focuses on youth empowerment, building stronger communities and providing support for families affected by drug addiction. She lives in Colleyville, Texas and is married to her college sweetheart and former NFL defensive back, Kevin Mathis. They are the proud parents of three children, Kennedy, Kaleb and Kole. She enjoys interior design, traveling, writing and a good book.

Table of Contents

Introduction

Born a dope baby, I became a college graduate, a mother of three, an entrepreneur, an Income Tax professional and an NFL wife. I was raised in the 80's and 90's amid the crack cocaine epidemic, the worst and deadliest drug surge the United States had ever seen that plagued predominantly low-income African American communities. This is a story of how the cheap drug caused devastating effects not only to the addict we come to know as Rose, but also to me, Rose's youngest child.

Almost every encounter we have with a person who suffers from addiction focuses primarily on their failed attempts to achieve sobriety, a typical life of crime to support their habit, and in some positive cases, their re-acclimation back into society and the monstrous task of maintaining a drug free life. We almost never dissect what the family of an addict experiences. I felt moved to write this book to offer a deep and personal look into how drug addiction has detrimental effects on the family members of addicts as well, particularly their children. This is my story. Let's rummage through every human emotion from fear and terror, to hope and despair, and finally freedom. This book will help you embrace your own life's challenges and learn to shed the shame of circumstances you couldn't or can't control, as you navigate how to live with other people's choices.

-Kimberly D. Mathis

Dope Girl

*A story of addiction.
A mother's struggle and the
baby girl she left behind.*

Written By:
Kimberly D. Mathis

"Dope Baby *(noun) - when a pregnant woman takes* **drugs** *such as heroin, cocaine, codeine, oxycodone (Oxycontin), methadone, or buprenorphine. These and other substances pass through the placenta that connects the* **baby** *to its mother in the womb. The* **baby** *becomes dependent on the* **drug** *along with the mother.*

"Children are often the silent victims of drug abuse."
- Rick Larsen

"The two most important days in your life are the day you are born, and the day you find out why." - Mark Twain

CHAPTER I
DOPESICK

It was Monday, May 15, 2000. Instead of celebrating the single greatest achievement of my young life, I found myself driving to downtown Dallas to the Greyhound bus station for only the second time. The first time was when my college roommate and I jumped on the bus, bright-eyed, full of excitement, with bikinis and flip flops packed and wearing sunglasses on the top of our heads, anxious to escape the stress of our grueling midterms. We were headed to Daytona Beach, Florida, with high hopes of soaking up some sun while blasting our favorite hip-hop anthems and having the best spring break ever as college sophomores. On this day though, I was facing yet another painful truth, I was picking up my mom. She was being released from the Hilltop Prison Unit of the Texas Department of Corrections. This was the second time. As I pulled up to the bus station and reluctantly walked inside to find a place to stand so she could find me, the only thing I could think of was how creepy the place was. It was dirty, it possessed such a coldness and there were numberless homeless people and drug addicts bombarding me with requests for spare change. It went something like, "Hey sis, you got any spare change or a couple of dollars I can have." A line I had heard more times than I cared to recall, except it had come from the woman I was there waiting to pick up, and the word "sis" was interchanged with "daughter". Those words ring like loud school bells in my ear, "Hey daughter, you got any spare change or a couple of dollars I can have" and add to it "I know your daddy gave you some money." Two years prior I guess I hadn't really noticed the obvious dump this place was, all I could see were the blue waves of the ocean, the warm sand and all the fruity drinks we wanted, virgins of course, that were waiting for us on the Florida beach. Just two days earlier, on Saturday, May 13, 2000, I had graduated from Texas A&M University-Commerce with a Bachelor of Business Administration ready to take on the world. My mom wasn't there. She had just missed it. Absent again, as it always seemed.

I was the only person in my family to graduate from college and it was being drowned out by mom's release. Although I was over the moon that I had accomplished such a massive four-year task of writing papers, taking exams, falling asleep in the library, skipping the occasional shower burning the midnight oil to get it all done, and becoming the latest expert on marketing strategies and accounting techniques, I wasn't up for much celebrating. Don't get me wrong, I was happy that mom was home, she had yet another chance to finally get it right, but I wanted out of the business of getting my hopes up, of at long last having a traditional mother-daughter relationship that never previously existed. Was this going to be another one of those times when she let me down? How long before she relapsed? How long before I get the dreaded call with the operator on the other line saying, "This is the Dallas County Jail, you have a collect call from Rose, do you accept?" By this time, I was three weeks shy of my 22nd birthday and I simply didn't have the space to digest another disappointment. "Kim, hey baby", came joyfully from across the room as mom made her way off the bus and into the waiting area. With a slight limp, she walked briskly towards me, arms stretched, about fifty pounds heavier and a head full of gray. She looked good. She looked healthy. She looked free. We embraced and hugged for so long that time certainly seemed to have stood still. I hadn't seen her or touched her in five years. And suddenly, the creepy bus station was the best place on earth.

I remember that day like it was yesterday. She had on khaki pants and a plain white shirt, both of which seemed oversized. That outfit was screaming "penitentiary",

"inmate", "jailbird", or whatever you wish to call it, and my next thought was, how fast can we get to the mall? But what was increasingly more painful than the outfit that spoke obvious volumes of a woman who had lived a life of hard knocks, was the single white trash bag she was carrying. It was the visualization that mom's entire life and worldly possessions had been reduced to only that trash bag. Her release papers, the conditions of her parole, an outfit that was obviously too small, a few letters and pictures, a small bag of toiletries, a tube of lipstick and some sanitary napkins filled the bag. It was all she currently owned and all she had to show for her then 44 years of life. I grabbed the bag, threw it in the car and drove away from the bus station for what I had hoped was the last time.

As we headed to see family and friends at my aunt's house, I asked mom about her recovery. "So, mom, how have you been? You're looking good, what are your plans for staying sober this time?" In her low raspy voice, accented with a slight southern drawl she replied, "Thanks baby, I'm good. I gotta go to those meetings. I'm staying clean this time, you don't have to worry about that." As much as I wanted to believe her, I just didn't. That was her victory yell every time she was released from jail, the penitentiary or the halfway house. Those words came from the pure emotion of finally being free and not having to deal with life's challenges, just yet. They must have been on repeat in her mind, like a favorite album or something. Only time was going to really tell, as it always does. And it never seemed to be on her side.

Before I knew it, the conversation had taken a sharp left. I think talking about her drug use in her sober state of mind made her uncharacteristically vulnerable. **Seemingly out of nowhere she said, "The day you were born the doctors came in the room and asked me what drugs I had been using. I didn't lie, I told them both heroin and cocaine."** She offered this revelation without any prompting or prying by me. Suddenly, my emotions were stagnant, I felt total numbness, this must be what it's like for her to get high, as I truly felt like I was having an out of body experience. We were about five miles past my aunt's house when I realized I was driving in the wrong direction and finally snapped back to reality. Did she just admit to my face that she chose to shoot heroin and use cocaine during her pregnancy to feed her selfish desires, more than she cared about how what she was doing was going to affect me? Though I had heard this before, it felt particularly damning to hear the words from her mouth.

Those words fell off her lips like hail falling from the sky, they were heavy, cold, and damaging. Really hitting hard and landing right in my heart, making yet another small dent. After a little self-talk, "Kim, you can handle this", and the feeling of excruciating chest pain, I said aloud, "Wow, you told them that!?" "Yep, I sure did, there was no need for me to lie, they knew anyway", she said with a straight face and a very matter of fact kind of tone. Followed by a somber, "I'm sorry baby." In the minutes that ensued before we arrived at my aunt's house, the silence in the car was deafening. My subconscious was taking me to a place of disbelief, anger and pity all at the same time. I can't believe she just said that! We all knew I was born a dope baby, there was no way to ignore the obvious, it was like an 800 pound gorilla in the middle of the room. Why didn't she just leave well enough alone? Doesn't she know that her drug use has hurt me enough? The cuts were finally starting to heal, and here she was picking at the scab. Yet somehow, her brazen honesty was refreshing, saying it aloud was a way to

35

recognize the mistake, the immeasurable pain it caused, and it opened the door for healing. Suddenly, I felt sorry for her. She must have said those words a thousand times in her head in the 1,825 days most recently spent in her Gatesville penitentiary cell. So, to tell them to my face must have taken all the guts she could muster. I appreciated her transparency, but only God knows how deep the wounds of her drug use and absence were, and I was leaning on him in that moment to help me see beyond my pain and allow myself to do for her what she had never done for me, be there when she needed me most.

We walked up the steps to my aunt's apartment. There was a birthday party going on for my little cousin, I think he was turning three. This would be the first time she had seen her nephew since he was born. The apartment was filled with music, party streamers, balloons, hot dogs and a cake. Although the party was for my cousin, and it just so happened to be on the day she was being released from prison, I'm sure she felt like it was a welcome home party, nonetheless. Her mom was there, two of her three sisters, one of her three living brothers, my sister, a few nephews and her grandkids. It was like a family reunion of sorts.

It was loud, and amongst the games of twister and pin the tail on the donkey, the only thing truly visible in the room was her smile. Her cheek bones were as high as I'd ever seen them as she grinned from ear to ear, elated to be surrounded by family and finally free. As we ate, danced and took plenty of pictures, thoughts of "can she do it" totally consumed me. I observed as she mingled through the room and played with the kids,

desperately hoping that she would get it right this time. I was trying to allow myself to be in the moment, to enjoy her genuine happiness and new-found freedom. But

my mind was six months down the road, to a woman who could very well be a shell of the person that we were seeing on that day. It had happened too many times before for this time to be any different, but I was hopeful. As I had been my entire life. As we left the party, I did something I had never done before. I took

37

mom home with me. During that time, I was engaged to my college sweetheart, ten months away from our wedding and living in a house he had recently purchased for us as a couple. We had plenty of room for mom. I was ecstatic for her to see all the awesome things going on in my life, my recent college graduation, my new home, the wedding we were planning and my new job I was about to start as a research analyst for a major corporation. It was icing on the cake that my sweetheart was living out his dream as a defensive back for our beloved Dallas Cowboys and I couldn't wait to take my mom to his games. As simplistic as it seemed, that was always a sore spot and a dream

of mine. Even though mom and dad weren't married, I wanted to have both my parents at the games too. It was a ritual for players' families to meet them in the family area after all the

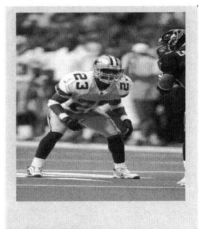

games. My trips down there were with all of my sweethearts' friends, his mom, his dad and my dad. My dad was a Cowboys super fan, so he was already going to the games, but now he was enjoying the perks of his soon-to-be son-in-law by visiting the family area and rubbing shoulders with some of his favorite players and the game's greats.

Our new house was a small two-story, with three-bedrooms. I fixed up one of the upstairs bedrooms with pale yellow floral bedding, complete with fluffy pillows, plush rugs, a TV and flowers. I figured the brightness of the room and the fresh flowers would give mom a sense of peace. It was my hope that it would brighten her spirits and create the imagery of a garden, providing calmness. It would have been a great escape from the one-inch thin mattress, paper-like blankets, concrete floors and bars she had grown accustomed to in her cell. Our house was nothing to brag about, it was cute, quaint and located in a nice neighborhood, but I'm sure it felt like a mansion to her. She even said, "What y'all gonna do with this big ole house, it's like a mansion." The bathroom probably felt like a mansion compared to the six by eight foot cell she had been in. My response, "We're gonna live in it mama, you should try to enjoy it." Home ownership was not something that had taken place much in my family. In fact, my entire life I had lived in an apartment. This was my first house too. And the thought of it was still surreal. In the last twenty-two years, the only places I could remember mom living were places with bars, a halfway house for addicts, the shelter and the alley close to my sister's apartment in the North Dallas projects. No place any mom should be, but her decision to self-medicate with illegal drugs and the life of crime she led to support her deadly habit, forced her down that repetitious path.

But today was a new day. All we could do was take it one step at a time as we attempted to work through the awkwardness of our broken relationship in this new space. Was she going to try to start "mothering" or "parenting" a twenty-two-year old college grad in her own house? Or was she going to take on the role of a friend? Neither of those things fully materialized, as we had a unique assimilation of the two. I can recall one time in the kitchen when I was cooking chicken fried steak. A dish I had made at least fifty times before. She went on to tell me how to season the meat, what I should have battered it with and even how long to cook it on each side. She eventually took the fork out of my hand and took over. I happily stepped aside and let her have her way. In the kitchen we laughed about what I was experiencing at my new job and how bored she had been all day. This scene was something I had envisioned in my head, but now that it was playing out, it felt somewhat dreamlike. On one hand, she was a mother, cooking for her family. And on the other, she was like my girlfriend I was venting to about new co-workers. It was a weird place to be. I don't remember many conversations with her beyond a 30 minute jailhouse or penitentiary visit behind a glass window, or a quick dash into my sister or my aunt's apartments in the projects to either change clothes, beg for money or food. We didn't have the history together for her to know that she didn't have to tell me how to cook that meal, grandma already had, or for her to really speak to where I was as a twenty-two-year-old navigating the growing pains of someone brand new to corporate America. Her absence made those simple life moments more difficult than they needed to be and neither of us deserved its emotional rigor. By the time a young woman reaches the tender age of twenty-two, you desire more of a friendship with your parents, and for girls, especially their

41

mothers. The perfect relationship is a great balance between the two: mother and friend. But Rose and I skipped past all the formative years of growth and character development. We were figuring it all out in my kitchen for the very first time.

The "mansion" as she called it, was located in Lewisville, Texas. We spent the following days trying to give mom a sense of normalcy in her new community. She didn't know much about the area, although it's only about 30 minutes outside of Dallas, she overreacted like she was in a foreign country or something. On the first Saturday that mom was with us following her release, I suggested that we go to the mall. It was definitely time to splurge on some new clothes, and not the Walmart threads she had been sporting all week. Rather grudgingly, she went. We walked through the mall with pretzels in tow, making our way into several stores. "This is cute, do you like this?" is the catchphrase I found myself echoing every five minutes. Only to be countered with, "That's cute, but baby I'm not gonna let you spend that much money on that." No amount of me saying, "It's really ok" would suffice. We were talking about stuff that was $20. And $20 to a lifelong drug addict was a "big hit" or "score". I guess she just wasn't as excited as I was about shopping. After about an hour, we made our way out of the last store and I asked, "Are you ok? What's the problem?" Her rebuttal was bleak, and something I was completely unprepared for. With what appeared to be a consciousness of humiliation, she said, "Being in this mall puts me on edge. I've never been in one to actually shop before." At that moment, the bitter absoluteness of mom's life was hitting me like a freight train traveling at top speed. I knew exactly what she was saying. My heart broke into a million pieces, as I stood there frozen with sorrow. Mom was being crippled and starved from the ordinariness of simply shopping because the hard realism was, she had never stepped foot into a mall in over 20 or so years, except to steal stuff and sell it for drug money. The mall was simply a place of resource for her. It was the way to her next hit. The action of walking into the mall with money to purchase anything she wanted without stealing it was more pressure than she could bear that day. It was painful and miserable to watch as I witnessed just how deprived she was of basic commonality. She felt nervous and ashamed. I felt it too. And it hurt like hell.

In a last-ditch effort to make something of the day, I suggested we see a movie. I threw out the titles of several new films playing at the time at a theater by the "mansion", but none of them were tempting enough. "Baby, I haven't been to the movies in 20 years either", she said dismally with a distinct expression of sadness. After gazing into her eyes for a moment, I watched as her emotional lights flickered out. Her shoulders relaxed and her head lowered in remorse as a deep sigh departed her mouth.

To put it plainly, that was just about as long as I had been alive. Something so elementary seemed almost unfathomable. Without her uttering another word, I knew what she meant about that too. Going to the movies was a two-fold issue. First, because she was a drug addict of the worst kind, her days were filled with nothing but the pure obsession of getting high and whatever that meant to do it. She could never be still long enough or have the money to go to the movies, nor did she want to when drugs were the single most important priority. Besides, I've never known movies to be a favorite pastime of addicts. Second, I think the darkness of the theater was frightening. It was purely symbolic of the dark places she had been, in jail, the alley and crack houses. How did we get here? A day that started with such promise, of a mother and daughter trying to develop a relationship and bond over shopping and a movie, resulted in neither. But it did expose the mountain of pain we had to climb. Though I often partake in going to the mall and the movies, neither will ever look the same to me again.

As the next few days passed, and we found ourselves getting into more of a routine, comprised of cooking dinner, talking and watching TV, her temperament seemed to change. She appeared antsy, anxious and uncomfortable. She started making plans to go back to Dallas because she wanted to see her sister and her grandkids. At least that was the excuse she gave. All of whom lived in the North Dallas projects, or Roseland Homes for formality's sake. Visiting the family wasn't a problem, in fact, I was willing to take her anytime she was ready, and happily. But I wasn't sold on the premise of her going by herself or me leaving her there. I just didn't trust her that much yet and I'm certain she didn't really trust herself all that much either. It was far too soon in her release. She hadn't really started

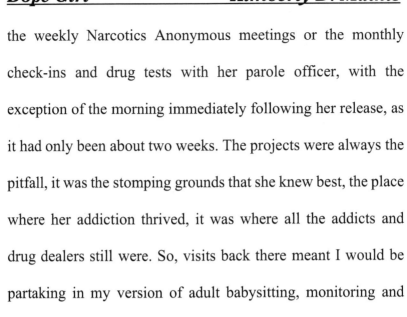

the weekly Narcotics Anonymous meetings or the monthly check-ins and drug tests with her parole officer, with the exception of the morning immediately following her release, as it had only been about two weeks. The projects were always the pitfall, it was the stomping grounds that she knew best, the place where her addiction thrived, it was where all the addicts and drug dealers still were. So, visits back there meant I would be partaking in my version of adult babysitting, monitoring and trying to keep an eye out to save her from any plethora of temptations that were always present.

I arrived home from work that Friday, with an arm full of pizza, Dr. Pepper, and a few DVD's. Poised for a weekend of binge watching all of the movies she had never seen during her imprisonment. Normally, crossword puzzle in hand, she would be sitting in the living room or at the white glass table in the kitchen. But that evening, she wasn't in either place. I raced upstairs to her room, confidently thinking I would find her resting or maybe taking a shower. But to my surprise, she was gone. The room was empty, and all that remained was the pale-yellow bedding and the TV. My heart sunk. The room with the garden presence, in the "mansion", was no place Rose wanted to be anymore. I knew where she had gone. And I knew this would be the beginning of the woman I had envisioned in my head six months down the road, just two weeks prior at my cousin's party. The pure terror that engulfed me that day was indescribable. I was fearful for her and scared to death. I knew in my gut this would be the start of yet another downfall. I stood in the doorway of what had been her room, lifeless and still as a statue, before finally falling to my knees and burying my tear-filled face on the carpet. How did I not see this coming? What did I expect? Why did I get my hopes up? And a thousand more similar questions swirled around in my head. God, I desperately wanted to try and help her make it this time. To give her a real fighting chance with a support system, finances and a home. This felt like a sucker punch to the stomach, and I learned that day that I wanted her sobriety, health and success far more than she actually did. My theoretical conclusion is simple. The suburbs were too slow for her, and she felt threatened by what a successful life without drugs in a new environment could be. It would take too much work. She wasn't prepared to have myself and my sweetheart hold her accountable for her actions and be intentional about her success. The thought of actually being better and doing better was a lot for her to manage. It was a desolate but very real existence. Like every other attempt at it was on her own, unchecked and unsuccessful.

I was convinced that she liked being undisciplined and unaccountable to anyone, it was her way of not taking full responsibility and facing life's challenges head on. I quickly realized that I had to consider what the core of the issue actually was. As truth would have it, addiction is nothing short of a brain disease. Though a self-inflicted one, a brain disease, nevertheless. Mom was living with a brain disease. The drugs had completely changed the chemical makeup of her brain, she had very little control of her choices, her actions and even how she felt. I wish I could tell you what triggered her to take a hit for the very first time, what was she trying to escape at such a young age? I was born when she was only twenty-two, and by then she was already a full-blown junkie. This perpetual cycle must have started in her late teens. Who was the loser that introduced it to her in the first place? The one thing about mom's tumultuous battle with drugs that still baffles me to this day is this: how could she go so long behind bars, free from drugs and their inevitable despair, and turn back almost immediately after being freed? She found the strength and willpower to stay clean for momentous periods of time, obviously because she had to behind bars, but didn't she like the feeling of being sober minded? Free to think for herself, free to learn, to grow and mature? My instincts tell me that she worked harder behind bars because she knew her binges and highs were logistically and physically impossible, and she was setting herself up for release. She looked like a model prisoner, working hard at rehabilitation. Once the release became a tangible sensibility, she allowed herself to have feelings she had deeply suppressed. The urges must have increased in rapid succession like the Texas heat, as logistical and physical barriers were no longer present. I wish like hell mom had tried that hard to stay clean at the "mansion". I wish she had just let us be there. I wish she could've finally overcome her demons. When my sweetheart came home that night, not a single word left my mouth, as my face told him everything he needed to know. My eyes were puffy as cotton

49

balls and candy apple red, and my face was covered with visible tear marks that showcased the pain. This was a very different and unnerving experience for him, as he was a country boy who had grown up in a home with both parents. His mom was home every day, she was at all of his football and basketball games, she cooked all the meals and her house was the one all the neighborhood kids hung out at. But for the first time, he was able to see what the previous twenty-two years had been like for me.

The days to follow were harder than any others, succeeding one of mom's disappointments. I had been let down limitless times before, but this time was different. This time I had really tried. I wasn't in a position previously to really do much, as I was just a kid. I was sixteen when she got locked up this last time, still walking through the halls of my high school and studying for algebra tests. My dad and grandma were still taking care of me. I had no job, no home, no resources. Nothing to offer mom. But at twenty-two, with a college degree, a new job, a new home, a sweetheart more than willing to offer love and support and finances to help, I was in the perfect position to pitch my mom a fastball so she could hit a home run. But none of that happened. I had the ball in my hand, but she never stepped up to the plate. She ran right past home and way out into left field. Opportunity can't tell time, and no time was more paramount than this, for her to do an about-face and allow change and possibility to cut into the rhythmless, never-ending slow dance she was having with drugs and life as she knew it.

The weeks and months flew by and I didn't hear a word from her. I went about my days tasting cake samples, making gift registries, picking out centerpieces and finalizing music selections for my upcoming wedding. I picked up right where I had left off, as if those two weeks with mom had never existed. I was good at blocking stuff out at this point and figuring out how to move on. The details were set, we decided on lavender and silver as our colors, the ceremony was being held at The Hall of State, the cake was white chocolate raspberry and the groom's cake was strawberry. The day had finally come, we were getting married! It was March 31, 2001. I arrived on site at about 4pm that afternoon. The ceremony was set to begin at 7pm. I spent the last few hours getting touch ups on my makeup, big curls in my hair and trying to breathe in my tight diamond

and pearl corset dress. My bridesmaids were with me, and Lynn, the wedding planner, was running frantically back and forth, checking on me and the guests. When the ceremony started, I stood at the back of the long 30-yard isle and gasped with happiness at the beauty of the room and the 400 guests that filled

it. I chose a non-traditional song to walk down the aisle to, but something that seemed more befitting of our love story. Stevie Wonder's, "Ribbon in the Sky." The music began, and the guests stood, trying to get a glimpse of me as I passed by. The walk down that aisle seemed endless. When I reached the very last row of seats before my dad gave me away, something on my left caught my eye. It was Rose. She was sitting on the second row with several other family members, dressed in lavender just as everybody else was to match our theme. She had a slight grin on her face, and she looked proud. After the ceremony was over, the bridal party and family members gathered for photos. My hubby hadn't noticed Rose at the wedding before it started, but let's unfold the devastating moment when he did.

We took pictures with his family and it was time to take pictures with mine. The photographer called everybody up, and as people proceeded, he looked at me and said, "Who's that?" With pain in my heart and a feeling of embarrassment, I said, "That's my mama." I will never forget the startling look he had on his face, Rose looked like a sick patient walking the tightrope of death. She was painfully thin. She was clearly strung out again, as the drugs had gotten the best of her once rounded physique. This was only the second time my hubby had ever met my mom; the first time was the day I picked her up from the Greyhound bus station and brought her back to the "mansion". I had been here before, it was a place I feared would come. But my new hubby didn't know what to think. Rose was indeed a shell of the person she was just ten months prior, she was at least 50 pounds smaller, her face was frail and jaws sunken in, her dress was too big and the wig she was wearing was covering her eyes. She was always a beautiful dark shade of ebony, but due to her obvious drug use, her skin appeared much darker than it should have been. I simply couldn't believe my eyes. We hadn't seen her since she disappeared from the "mansion". We had no communication with her either. I stood there stunned and wildly puzzled. How did she even know where the wedding was? Who

told her? She and I never got to discuss those details. Where did she get that dress? That wig? My feelings were all over the place. I suspected she had stolen those items, but I was

pleased that she had tried to pull herself together to be there for me that day. It must have taken her an enormous amount of strength to get cleaned up, to find clothes, and shoes, whether they were stolen or not and a ride there. She put in a great effort with where she was at that point, that was clear. She even painted her nails and wore a necklace. On the other hand, I felt ashamed. There were a lot of prestigious people in that room, from bankers and doctors to attorneys and world-famous athletes. What were they going to think? Most of them had no idea she was my mom, or who she was at all. Maybe the fear of people knowing who she was, was all in my head. Maybe it wasn't. Either way, my mind was definitely going in circles, about as frantically as a dog chasing its own tail. **But you are as sick as your secrets, and my wedding wasn't the day I wanted my sickness to show.** We finished the pictures and headed to the dance floor. We spent the next three hours dancing, cutting cake and mingling with guests. Exhausted and my feet throbbing in pain, we darted from the reception and made our way to the limo. It was getting late and we had an early flight out the next morning. We gave hugs and waved goodbye. As the limo took off, we were gone and so was Rose. We were headed for a new life together that should have had her in it. My best guess, she was headed back to more destruction.

> "You are as sick as your secrets."

Sister Friend (noun) - Better than any friend. More like family. Who's been your friend for so long you **might as well** be sisters.

"Not sisters by blood, but sisters by heart." – unknown

CHAPTER 2
SISTER FRIEND

It was August 1989. I was eleven years old and it was the first day of fifth grade. Holy Trinity Catholic School was new to me. I had spent the previous five years at St. Peter's School. I'm not sure why my dad decided to change my school, I had made friends and was looking forward to being on a different side of the building where all the other fifth grade classes were. The fifth graders were the "big kids". I think my dad's decision had something to do with how close this school was in proximity to his job. I really don't have a definitive answer, but I was somewhat cheerful though. May dad always picked me up from school, but on the days he couldn't make it, my older cousin would come to get me and we would make the

57

ten-minute walk from St. Peter's back to my aunt's apartment in the projects. That walk was brutal. In my navy-blue uniform jumper, crisp white shirt and blue and white saddle oxfords, I

walked under the bridge and past more homeless people and drug addicts than you'd ever want to see. Looking down the whole time, trying to avoid stepping on any of the empty liquor bottles, used needles and crack pipes scattered on the ground. Trash was everywhere, old disgusting furniture, and makeshift houses made from cardboard boxes.

Shopping carts were present too, they were stacked with everything from bags of aluminum cans, to old stereo speakers and useless electronics. What was the point of all that stuff? The cans I know were sold for money, as my grandma had trained me to pick up any cans I laid my eyes on. She had a huge black trash bag in her trunk full of them. The scene reminded me of

58

something I had seen on TV in a third world country. It was filthy, and reeked of the worst odors, a combination of pee, alcohol and dog feces. I hated making that walk from school. It was all so depressing. Every now and then I would let my eyes drift up to see if this was a day that I would spot my mom amongst the hopelessness. I had seen her under that bridge several times before and it was heartbreaking. I got nervous when I looked up, secretly praying that I would be let down. A disappointment I happily welcomed.

We emerged from the bridge and walked by the corner store. Sometimes we stopped and loaded up on pickles, chips, candy and soda. We finished the track by walking past an alley diagonally across from the store. To me, passing that alley felt like my last event of an obstacle course. That's because I was hoping to walk by that alley and not see my mom there either. If I made it past the bridge and the alley without seeing her, whew, that was a major feat! It was like a little game I played with myself. As I clutched the straps of my backpack, I would cross my fingers for good luck, hiding them so no one would see. If she wasn't under the bridge, I would do a little skip, if she wasn't in the alley, I would do two skips. Once I made it past both, I uncrossed my fingers in relief and skipped the rest of the way to my aunt's apartment, leaving my cousin behind. My cousin never knew why I was skipping so jubilantly, I felt like I had won a grand prize and was showing off my celebratory dance. Silly, I know. But in my eleven-year-old mind it made all the sense in the world. It was how I coped with having an addict for a mom. The days when I was able to skip the rest of the way were indeed self-gratifying victories. At my new school, I wasn't going to ever have to worry about making that heart stopping walk, it was too far away. Dad had to pick me up. Sometimes I stayed in the after-school program if he couldn't make it. I hated it at first, but it turned out not to be so bad. They had good snacks and I could finish my homework and then go play outside for the rest of the time. That meant less time to stay in the projects and no chance of walking under the bridge.

The situation is somewhat complex. I lived with my maternal grandma in a two-bedroom apartment in a crime ridden urban area of Southeast Dallas commonly referred to as Pleasant Grove. But before Pleasant Grove we lived in Oak Cliff.

Basically, going from a semi decent area of blacks doing well and living above the poverty line, to an area where a portion of the apartments were classified as Section 8. No doubt the living conditions changed. Grandma was a calm spirited woman, full of wisdom and plenty of stories of the days she spent picking cotton. She bore nine children and lived out her days as a nanny and housekeeper for an affluent white family.

I had mad cleaning skills and every now and then I would go to work with her and transform the upstairs bedrooms from disastrous to miraculous. She would pay me $20, a respectable $10 a room, and I'd be pretty satisfied. Sometimes on our way home, she  would stop at the store and let me run inside to get a treat. That $20 was burning my pocket and I was looking forward to a reward. She enjoyed card parties and would often drag me with her to the bingo hall. Since my mom was in no position to take care of me, my grandma graciously did, and I lived with her and my uncle until his sudden death. My uncle was the sparkle in my eyes. I have vivid memories of him buying me pretty dresses with petticoats and matching bows for my hair. And if I got

fussed at for leaving my toys all over the place or my bike in the middle of the walkway, I would run straight to his arms for comfort. He dyed Easter eggs with me and would always partake in my

childish practice of playing school. He, Strawberry Shortcake and Rainbow Brite were always my best students. My uncle was an active citizen and often took me with him when he volunteered on campaigns for candidates running for the Dallas City Council. I found myself at the campaign headquarters, stuffing envelopes and walking the streets placing flyers in the residents' mailboxes. He was like my best friend. He died when I was about nine years old and everything seemed to change. Or maybe I changed because my heart was so broken. Losing my uncle was the single greatest loss I had ever experienced. After his death, it was pretty much just me and grandma.

Because both grandma and my dad worked, I had to have a place to go when school let out. That place was my aunt's house. She happened to live in the projects. Once my grandma left her job, she would pick me up and we headed home. It was the strangest set of dynamics. My mother was an addict and I was a uniform wearing private school girl, who lived in the hood. I attended school with upper class white folks by day and lived amongst poverty-stricken blacks by night. I guess you could say I had the best of both worlds. Even though I was struggling to find the best parts of the hood. It was literally from one extreme to the other, like two different worlds existed.

On the first day of fifth grade I showed up to Holy Trinity in a green plaid jumper with navy, red and yellow stripes and a pale-yellow shirt underneath. We wore navy knee high socks and saddle oxfords here too. I walked into the classroom scared and doubtful. Looking around to find my name on the desk, I noticed another black girl. She was brown skinned with

63

long ponytails and bright eyes. We made eye contact and she gave me a smile. As I realized that she wasn't the only black girl in the class, my uncertainty quickly turned to joy. It was something about seeing faces that looked like me that gave me comfort. I didn't know much about this place, but I was starting to like it already. I think it ended up being four of us black kids in that class. All of us girls. This was definitely odd, we weren't just in a private school, but a Catholic school. It wasn't a whole lot of black folks doing the Catholic school thing. This meant nuns, weekly mass, saying Hail Mary's with a rosary and reciting the beatitudes, the whole nine. It was a far cry from my traditional Baptist upbringing of praise dancing, foot stomping and tambourine playing. Those were all just formalities of receiving a top education, as we weren't there for the religious practices, we got tons of that at our own churches, it was purely an education thing.

At lunch on that first day the girl with the bright eyes introduced herself to me. She said, "Hi, my name is LaTonya, but you can call me Tonya." "Hi, I'm Kim", I answered. Tonya already seemed more outspoken than me and she was no nonsense too. Later, on the playground I saw her yelling at someone for trying to take the ball we were playing with. She got all in that little boy's face, hid the ball behind her back and firmly said, "Try to take it from me." Immediately, I knew we would be friends and we were going to have a great year. I was quiet that day as I was trying to take it all in, but I'm naturally feisty and once Tonya got to know me, we would be a playground wrecking ball duo. My mouth and her attitude, aw shucks, look out! As the weeks passed and our class got into a daily routine, the more comfortable we got with each other, the sillier the kids got. On one particular day, I wore my hair up in a high bun. Every time I turned my back two boys in my class thought it would be a good idea to stick pencils in my bun. They were pointing and laughing uncontrollably. Tonya caught them, yelled at them and made them take those pencils out. Let's just say, when she got finished with them, they weren't laughing but were on the verge of tears themselves. Man, this girl was tough! She didn't play and everybody in fifth grade knew it. I was a short kid for my age, and everybody was always testing me. Little did they know, I really wasn't the one to mess with. I had seen more disappointments and been through more heartache than all of them combined, so I could totally hold my own. You don't get to be a project kid and not develop tough skin. It was virtually impossible. Still, picking on me just wasn't going to happen as long as Tonya was around, and she inadvertently became my protector.

There was another time when the same two boys who had been caught putting pencils in my hair thought it would be cool to make up a rap song about me. It was styled after the first verse of the 1986 Run DMC hit "It's Tricky". It went something like, "I met this little girlie, her name was Kimmy Curlee, I went to her house and bust her out and had to leave her early." It was so aggravating. The verse itself eluded to a guy going to a girl's house to have sex and then abruptly leaving, basically getting what he wanted and abandoning her there. I honestly think they were too stupid to know what the song actually meant, they were just tickled by how my name rhymed with the words. They had all the boys singing it. Well, we know who put a stop to that. Yep, Tonya! I think her exact words were, "If y'all don't stop singing that song, I'm gonna bust y'all out!" Needless to say, we never heard that song again. A couple of months after school started, Tonya invited me to her house for a sleepover. She actually lived in some apartments directly across the street from my dad's apartment. That was an odd discovery. Her apartment was charming, and it had stairs inside. I thought that was so dope. The living room was so nicely decorated with a velvet-like brown sofa so beautiful that you didn't even want to sit on it. When I got to her house it didn't take me long to figure out why she was so tough. She was a latch key kid living with a single mother who worked two jobs and 80+ hours a week. She already knew how to ride the city bus on her own and how to cook a full course Sunday meal. I'm talking about meatloaf, greens, black-eyed peas and sweet potatoes. That was impressive! It was stuff my grandma would make. At that time, I only knew how to cook spaghetti and eggs. Unless we can count sandwiches. She was like a little woman, taking charge and helping her mom run the house. She even had the responsibility of dropping off the rent money at the office and paying the water bill with money her mom would leave on the kitchen table. She had duties of huge importance. Those boys were no match for this super girl. I had similar qualities. I was

being raised by a single father and grandma and I could clean

my butt off, better than any eleven-year old on the planet and

even better than most adults. Tonya and I grew very close. We

practically lived at each other's houses. We shared everything

from clothes to parents. We grew accustomed to this

unconventional family type situation. Her mother became a

stand in mom for me
and my dad was the
same for her. Though
we both had the other
parents, neither of them
was around. Tonya's
dad lived in another

state and my mom, well, we all know she lived on the streets. It

was bizarre by most people's standards, but it was functioning,

and it worked for us. I had her mom to talk to about boys, what

a menstrual cycle was like and even sex. Yep, we had those talks

pretty early. She would treat us girls to new hairdos at the beauty

college and all the ribs we could eat at Tony Roma's. My dad was equally as important to Tonya as he took us to all the Cowboys, Mavericks and Rangers games we could stand. He paid for us to go to summer camp and gave us both an allowance on Fridays. We couldn't wait to get our $20, we would spend it at the bazaar or on junk food and cheap earrings from the beauty supply store. Those were trying times, but they were filled with a lot of love and exactly what we needed.

On the Friday it was time for Tonya to spend the night at my house, she was subjected to my after-school routine too. That meant Dad would be waiting outside the school building to pick us up and take us to my aunt's house in the projects, where we would wait for grandma to come get us before finally heading home. On the way, dad would always make a stop at 7-Eleven and let us girls run inside and get the biggest Slurpee we wanted and all the snacks our little hands could carry. We each had a bag full of stuff. We would stand in the aisle and debate over what flavor of chips to get so we didn't grab the same kind and we could share. "I'll get barbeque!", I would exclaim. "Ok, I'll get sour cream", Tonya would say. We'd mosey out of the store and jump back into dad's car. If it was a nice day, we'd be rolling with the convertible top of his Camaro down. Imagine that, us

private school girls decked out in plaid uniforms and pulling up to the projects in a convertible. It was a real-life oxymoron,

projects, private school and convertible just didn't go together.

After we devoured chips, Butterfinger's and pickles with peppermints inside, we would run outside to play. The projects didn't offer much for us kids in terms of fun, with the exception of a broken-down swing set that had only one working swing and a basketball goal with no net. So, we made our own fun. We played tetherball, a game where we placed a ball in an old stocking and tied it to a pole. Hitting it back and forth until it finally wrapped all the way around the pole. Then there was the famous hide and seek game. We would all put our feet in a circle and cited the counting-out rhyme, "eenie, meenie, miney, moe, catch a tiger by its toe, if he hollers, let him go. My mother said to pick the very best one and you are not it." Us project kids

didn't say tiger though, we said monkey. It wasn't until later that I realized the racist undertone that rhyme had. It was originally written as, "eenie, meenie, miney, mo, catch a nigger by the toe, if he hollers, let him go." Nigger then monkey, we get the correlation and we see how America tried to clean it up. Sadly, the kids in the projects and on playgrounds all across the country were learning that rhyme. Once someone was designated as "it", we would scatter so fast to try and hide. We looked a lot like folks running to escape the sound of gunshots ringing out, but we were just playing, trying to find the best hiding place. It was reminiscent of the drive-by scene in the John Singleton movie, *Boyz n the Hood*. We ran under wire clothes lines and got screamed at a hundred times for knocking people's clothes down. We couldn't pick those clothes up fast enough and sprint off again to avoid being identified before the screaming voices emerged from the door. "Stay out of my yard. Don't run under my clothesline again!", is what the voices would say. And they could be coming from any number of places as there were clotheslines everywhere. We made a lot of childhood memories in the projects, it's what was necessary and required of us to

escape the complex palpability we were living with. After visiting my mom in prison once, the projects in a weird way reminded me of a prison. There was an aura of brokenness that

covered the place like a dark cloud. Similarly, both had metal and concrete everywhere. The floors in the projects were made of tile and dark gray concrete. The walls were even made of concrete. And the stairs too. The clotheslines outside reminded me of barb wire fencing, and cops strolled the place on foot and patrol cars, just like prison guards. There wasn't much intellectual or economic progress being made and symbolic of prisoners, everyone seemed stuck. If you ask me, there wasn't much difference between the two. It was confinement, and everything was being destroyed from the inside out. In the projects, the people were destroying each other. Stealing was rampant, fights broke out every day over stupid stuff like not returning a cup of borrowed sugar or someone's kid standing on someone else's porch, and not a day went by where we didn't see an ambulance. That meant someone had been shot and it was a toss-up as to if they would survive. Some people shot folks as a result of those heated arguments over unreturned sugar, as what was originally intended as a scare tactic foolishly became costly accidents. Obviously, someone went to the hospital and someone else went to jail. Those circumstances were so dumb. But it was the result of people using guns to settle any conflict, no matter how small. The silliest of reasons caused people to inflict vicious harm towards each other as egos and attitudes were larger than Big Tex himself, the humongous State Fair mascot that stands a towering 55 feet in the air because the fight for relevance was tense. Others were far more serious, and we would later find out that it was a drug deal gone bad or some territorial dispute with a gang. It was our assumption as to what had just taken place when we were forced to clear the yard for the ambulance to get through. I mean, the ambulance would drive right through the buildings and directly into people's yards. It was a wild scene every single day and all of that was taking place between our games of hide and seek and tetherball.

The criminal justice system was destroying people from the inside out too. Black people were going to jail at disproportionately higher rates than any other group. Thanks to Nixon's War on Drugs, implemented in 1971, where he declared, "Public enemy number one in the United States is drug abuse." This preposterous declaration targeted primarily at blacks was criminalizing drug use. Rose and addicts like her were a measured ingredient in this bitter recipe. It was a half-baked, cynical political tool that destroyed black America. And the lingering effects are very much visible to this day, as 1 in 9 black children have an incarcerated parent, compared to 1 in 57 white children, and a staggering amount are serving time for nonviolent drug law violations. The senseless drug war has been proven counterproductive and will forever be a dark stain on this country. This was not a war on drugs, but merely a war on people. It was designed to make freedom almost impossible. It was a set-up and it was working. Because let's be clear, our nation's cash bail system continues to be broken. This has

74

become a for-profit cash cow, and really crystallizes the perception that how much money you have is far more crucial than the nature of your crime and the risk you pose to society. If you can afford bail, they snatch the handcuffs off and let you go free. If you can't, the handcuffs hypothetically tighten. The real crime then becomes being too poor to buy your own freedom. And how on earth do you begin to fight a system that appears vehemently rigged against you? Fast forward to 2019, and the opioid crisis once again has become an epidemic, wiping out white America like a murderous tsunami. Now that the tides have turned, disturbingly, so has the conversation. Experts and lawmakers have suggested that opioid abusers need therapy, which is extremely maddening and ridiculously biased since blacks who were crack cocaine abusers needed jail. All addicts require a combination of both therapy and education, not incarceration. And skin color should not be a determining factor as it relates to treating the mental illness of addiction. Definitely not my idea of "liberty and justice for all." Black or white, the devastating effects remain the same. By now the street lights had come on, which was our que to come inside, as my grandma had arrived, and it was time for Tonya and me to go. We grabbed our backpacks and the plastic grocery sacks we had stuffed our uniforms in when we changed into our play clothes and headed towards the car. It was a quiet ride home as we were both exhausted. We were sitting on opposite sides of the back seat and each of our heads had found a resting place on the window. KHVN, a gospel station that grandma listened to was playing on the radio. It felt like we heard the words to "Uphold Me" by The Winans the whole way home. I could see grandma mimicking the words, "Uphold me with thy free spirit, whatever you do, Lord don't take your joy from me." That song and so many others like it are ingrained in my head. Gospel was all we listened to in grandma's car. And most of the time, it was all we had to make it through, whether the music was actually playing or not. We arrived at our apartment and sluggishly walked up the flight of stairs. I was simultaneously rambling through my backpack for the door key. Grandma had a burglar door installed. It was kind of weird. You don't usually see burglar bars on apartment doors, those were typically reserved for people with houses, but on our side of town and those apartments in particular justified one. Once inside I took Tonya to my room. It was the largest of the two bedrooms. It had a dresser and a chester drawer in it that had previously belonged to grandma, and twin beds with matching bedding that grandma had gotten from the affluent white family she was nannying for. There was also a wooden desk with a computer and a dot matrix printer on it that my dad had gotten for me to do my school work on. The walls were covered with posters of Salt-n-Pepa, New Edition and The Boys. We used to get them out of *Word Up*! magazine. My room was very different from Tonya's room. She had a complete bedroom set, where all the pieces matched. Her room had a black lacquer queen bed, dresser, armoire and nightstand. They were all trimmed in gold. It was beautiful. I'm not sure what she was thinking about my room. The furniture pieces weren't an exact match, but it worked.

  The next day, on Saturday, we went to the bazaar. It was like a cheap marketplace for clothes, shoes, jewelry and electronics. It was huge. We marveled over which pair of British Knights sneakers and Cross Colours outfits we were going to put on our Christmas lists. Girbaud jeans were very popular back then too, and I think we spent an hour trying on every pair. By the end of the weekend, we had watched Spike Lee's, *Do the Right Thing* so many times we could quote every scene. I had the voice of Tina, Rosie Perez's character down pact and Tonya was Spike Lee's character Mookie. We had a blast that weekend. It was all a much-needed distraction from the daily stress of worrying about mom. As the years passed, Tonya and I became inseparable. I was enamored by the fact that Tonya and I could tell each other anything. There was never any judgement between us. I shared with her all of my emotions about my mom. How on most days I was mad as hell at her, how I felt so unimportant to her and mostly how I was terrified to get a phone call that she was dead.

Tonya took on that pain. She carried it with her and lived it with me daily. She had seen mom at her worst many times and she just accepted it as just another part of me. I can remember a time in our teens when we were starting to date. We always seemed to like guys in the same friend circle. Maybe it was just easier for us, it wasn't like there were many times when we weren't together anyway. It usually worked out in our favor because we could always do the double date thing and use each other as an excuse. We had gone to my sister's house for the day, and we invited our new guy friends over to watch a movie. That in itself was all so taboo. Us two private school girls who had met boys at the mall were inviting them to the projects versus a house or even Tonya's apartment. Lord, what were these fellas going to think? And would they even come? This was dangerous for them, since they lived on the nice side of town. It's not like we had many choices. I lived too far away and neither my dad nor Tonya's mom was going to approve anyway. My sister was cool, and since we technically didn't have permission from our parents to have boys over, my sister's house it was.

While the four of us were sitting in the living room, the door flung wide open and my mom stumbled inside. Literally stepping over her own feet and shuffling along as she tried to keep her balance. She looked frightening and was in incredibly bad shape. I think she was coming off a binge or was smack dab in the middle of one. Her hair was scattered all over her head, her clothes were dirty, and she had an awful odor. I'm sure she hadn't bathed in days, maybe even a week. Who knows? Her face was very dark and covered with sores. She wobbled right past all of us and headed straight for the kitchen. She was rambling soft whispers of something, but I couldn't make sense of what she was trying to say. I was praying that she wouldn't call me or Tonya by name. Giving the guys any indication that we knew this homeless addict. That experience was both terrifying and embarrassing. Terror and embarrassment were emotions I just couldn't seem to escape. She grabbed something to eat from the kitchen and quickly left. She was there for maybe five minutes, but it felt like hours, as time always seems to stand still in hellish moments too. I'm sure it freaked the guys out. Their faces were filled with bewilderment and obvious distress. They both stood up, motioning to each other to leave. Just before walking out of the door, the brown skinned cutie with the perfect set of teeth that I called myself crushing on blurted out, "Who was that, some crackhead?!" The sound of those words was agonizing. He had no idea he was talking about my mom. And I sure as hell wasn't about to tell him. After the guys left, I sat on the couch and sobbed helplessly. Every time I saw her, she was getting progressively worse, leaving even more gruesome images in my mind and I was losing hope fast that she would ever get help. She was most certainly drowning on dry land. I think the only words that Tonya could let escape were, "It's ok Kimma." Kimma was the nickname she had given me. We both sat there, with our heads loosely forged together and our hands intertwined, momentarily staring into space and trying desperately to catch our breath. That experience had completely knocked the wind out of both of us. Just her sitting there with me was all the comfort I needed. Tonya was so much more than just a friend to me, she was family. I call her my sister friend.

*"**Dear God**"* (proper noun) - used for expressing strong emotion, especially anger, fear and shock.

*"**Dear God**,* I'm not asking you to make my life easier, I'm asking for the strength to face all my trouble."
- Kimberly Mathis

"When you love someone, you protect them from the pain, you don't become the cause of it." – unknown

CHAPTER 3
"*DEAR GOD*, PROTECT MAMA"

Twenty-two was a significant age for both me and mom. What we had accomplished by the time each of us had reached that mark in life was about as drastic as a dial-up versus a Wi-Fi internet connection. When Rose was twenty-two, her life was already in a spiral out of control, and it had apparently been trending that way for years. She could be identified as a high school dropout, an unwed mother of a seven-year-old and a pregnant junkie. She had no place to call her own, no job and her arrest record was taking on the shape of Pinocchio's nose. She was far too young to be in this destitute place. What led her here? Consequently, sometime between fifteen and twenty-two, did she become a teenage user? The thought of this seemed too extravagant to actually be real. But there must be some validity to it. As there's just no logical explanation as to how she had already reached the escalated maturation of her drug use if she had just begun in her early twenties before I was born. She was far too seasoned at it by then.

What I know to be true is this: drug addiction happens in four specific stages. First, there's experimentation, then there's regular use, followed by risky use and finally, you arrive at total dependency. She was well past dependency. Her habit had become completely compulsive and being pregnant for the second time was not about to change anything. What was she trying to escape? She was only fifteen when my sister was born, was the pressure of being a teen mom and school too much? People often turn to drugs in the most desperate of times. Without stating the obvious, I see just how desperate things must have been. She was just a kid herself. But was there more? Or was her introduction to drugs something recreational that got out of hand? I've always been unclear about what exactly started her self-destruction. Who introduced it to her? What were her triggers? I've tried to walk myself through her head to better understand her logic and how this all unfolded to get a glimpse of what life must have been like in the 60's and 70's for someone in her position. It's about as complicated as trying to do advanced physics.

Mom had a twin brother and I never knew their father. I didn't even know her to have a relationship with him at any point. He was my grandfather and even his name had been a mystery at first. I'm not exaggerating when I say, no one mentioned him. Ever. To know him would be to know her as well. It would provide insight as to her genetic and psychological make-up. Those things, coupled with what people accepted as social norms back then, play a major factor in her vulnerability towards addiction. Was he a drug user? An alcoholic? If so, that would make her highly more susceptible to addiction. As much as I want to believe mom's addiction was genetic in nature and I do believe it was somewhat, I think more of it was her personality. She was impulsive and impatient and quick on her feet. Her impulsivity was a crave for immediate satisfaction and responses, not delayed ones. In other words, she didn't want to wait for anything, her needs had to be fulfilled immediately. And that's what getting high did. Give immediate pleasure. This has never been more evident than when she stayed those two weeks at the "mansion." Her progress was steady, but slow. She was creating new norms, fostering new relationships and learning to trust herself again. All of which requires an extensive amount of time to master. There were no quick results. She had grown reliant on things happening fast. Patience just wasn't a virtue for her, and she bailed.

I can sharply recall a time when I was sitting at my aunt's kitchen table, doing my homework and mom walked through the door. I saw her walking up the sidewalk from the window. She seemed to be in a hurry, again. "Where's your auntie?", she asked. "Upstairs, I think", I replied. "Go tell her we'll be right back", she said eagerly. I ran up the stairs and told my aunt that my mom was downstairs, and we were going somewhere. She was just as shocked as I was. She said, "Who's downstairs?" Again, I said, "My mom". "And where are y'all going?", she asked. Confused, I stated, "I don't know". I could tell that my aunt was worried. She didn't trust me leaving with her, it was just too risky. However, neither of us wanted to deny that we could use a little time together. Surely, she wasn't crazy enough to do anything with her child in tow. Enthusiastically, I walked out of the door and followed behind as we walked down the sidewalk and got into a white van that was parked on the curb. Whose van was this? Where did she get it from? That van felt wrong from the minute my little fingers touched the door handle. It was very distinctly a work van. It was overflowing with buckets of cleaning supplies and loose mops and brooms. But who did it belong to? We took off and made a right at the stop sign. We drove maybe a mile down the road and pulled up to a clothing store. In another display of quickness, I watched as my mom walked past one aisle of baby clothes and down another. Occasionally glancing at the man who was sitting at the counter. The aisles were exceptionally long. She settled on a place right in the middle of the next aisle and took both of her hands and pushed clothes outward, leaving a bundle of clothes in the middle of the rack. She grabbed the bundle and stuffed about twenty outfits under her shirt. Giving the illusion of a pregnant belly. She even grasped the bottom of her shirt to hold the clothes in as if she was caressing an unborn child. Clearly, she had done this before. She walked out of that store faster than I had ever seen her move. We jumped into the van and drove off. I was mortified. I had just witnessed a theft. Maybe even a felony and I was an accessory. But what was even more disgraceful was the lack of shame she portrayed. My sole purpose for being there was to make her scheme look real. A mom with a kid and another on

> "I had just witnessed a theft. Maybe even a felony. And I was an accessory."

the way, it had all the makings of believability. I was there as a distraction and a prop. The man hadn't really noticed her when she first walked in and walking past the first aisle was a detail that made her look like she was genuinely searching for something. I'm sure the man wasn't concerned, as thieves don't typically come to steal with kids. She took me back to my aunt's house and dropped me off on the curb. My services were no longer needed. Even that mother and daughter moment was over as quick as it started. I was a quick means to an end. This was an inarguable pattern in mom's life. Running into a store to steal something "real" quick, a quick high or grabbing a quick bite to eat from my sister or my aunt's kitchen. To include quick jailhouse visits with me or whoever else would come. Even quick ways to clean up her appearance with a wig or a long sleeve shirt to cover the track marks on her arms. Everything was quick. Nothing at the "mansion" was happening quickly.

It also explains her reservations about the movies and the mall. Getting a full mall experience is not quick. You can't absorb all it has to offer in five minutes. You have to walk all the way through it. And the relationship she had with it was just to make a quick buck. The movies were much of the same. It's not possible to get through a movie quickly. It takes time to tell a story. Add to that the darkness her quick highs provided via prison and the streets. It all makes perfect sense now. Rose was just as much a victim of her own personality traits as she was to the critical circumstances or curiosity that led her to do drugs in the first place. By the time I had reached twenty-two, my life was extensively opposite, and my accomplishments could fill a page. Steadily and diligently I worked hard for everything. In high school I was a tour guide, a yearbook staffer, a three-year cheerleader, a member of the Spanish Club, Future Homemakers of America, and in computer cluster. Because I was a member

of the National Honor Society, that meant graduating with honors too. And proudly, I was headed to college on a full academic scholarship awarded through a prestigious foundation. College had plenty of successes of its own. Once I arrived, I became a collegiate cheerleader and participated for three years. I served as my sorority's president for two years and member of the year, and I was a frequent affiliate to the Dean's List. I even secured an internship at a local TV station in Dallas. Upon graduation, I accepted a position at a major corporation as a research analyst. Things were definitely looking bright. And let's not forget I was about to marry my college sweetheart. Life couldn't have been vastly more different for me and mom. Her absence had abhorrent effects on me though. That paired with

any number of other trials

that were present in my

life, could have led me

down a similar path to her.

But Rose's dysfunction

was the driving force

behind much of my

success.

Life Comparison Ages 15-22	
Kim	**Rose**
•Cheerleader	•Baby
•High School Graduate	•High School Dropout
•College Graduate	•20+ Arrests
•Corporate Research Analyst	•Drug Abuse
•Married	•Dope Baby

Long before all the accolades, my days were permeated

with more "Oh My God" moments than rightfully necessary. I

was a witness to the perils of addiction, her lack of self-respect

and motivation, her loss of dignity and her stifled intellectual

and psychological growth. As much as I tried to guard myself

against those struggles, it's undeniable that a parent's genetic

makeup, behaviors, habits and values shape our world

perceptions and ultimately our choices. But I refused to show

even the slightest resemblance to her. I'll be damned. It just

wasn't going to happen. I took a hard pass on the fruit from her

poisonous tree. Back to that atrocious moment in the store. It

91

was a perfect display of how differently we each viewed the world. I can't even explain how traumatic that experience was. She used me. All I wanted to do was spend some time with her. I was only eleven and I had been subjected to seeing her under the bridge and now committing crimes to feed her habit. I was crushed and authentically upset, I prayed that God would send her to jail that day. Over and over, I cried out, "God, this is not fair. Why me?" She was out of control and going to jail meant she couldn't hurt me again. We didn't think she would be foolish enough to put her own child in harm's way, but evidently, we didn't understand the depths of her desperation.

My Catholic school rituals kicked into high gear and I began praying my heart out. Reciting The Lord's Prayer continuously. "Our father, which art in heaven, hallowed be thy name. Thy kingdom come, thy will be done, on earth as it is in heaven. Give us this day our daily bread. And forgive us our trespasses, as we forgive those who trespass against us. And lead us not into temptation but deliver us from evil. For thine is the kingdom, the power, and the glory, forever and ever. Amen." It seemed fitting for what had just occurred. My childhood was blanketed with many dark days like that one. Yet and still, I had enormous sympathy and love for her. It was the kind of love that only a child could give. Love that was innocent. Love that was pure. Love that knew no boundaries. I was no different than any other kid who had found themselves suffering through the warfare of addiction, we would hurt and then we would forgive. No matter how tragic things got, I would always let her back into my heart. I was resilient, and I loved her. As flawed as she was, she was the mom God chose for me. Inevitably, my mom's reckless behavior started to manifest in my life in negative ways. I didn't trust people, I started to resent members of my family for not doing more to help her, and as I got older, I used my words as a weapon. My mouth was like a cannon, firing expletives at anyone who dared to try and hurt me. It's what I developed as a way to defend myself. I wasn't much of a fighter, but because of my mouth, I didn't have to be either. It paid dividends in the projects. I would hear, "You're such a pretty girl, until you open your mouth." That statement slapped me right in the face, but it was true. If only people knew where that pain was coming from. Of all the illegal and dangerous things mom did to keep her habit alive, I can convincingly conclude that none of her actions were a threat to public safety. She was discernibly a threat to herself. No action of stealing or attempting to distribute would lead her to cause physical harm to people as a whole. But emotionally and psychologically she was causing more harm than a Texas twister. Raging like a tornado's violent wind, hurting and destroying anyone in her path. Especially me. Just like she did when she took me into that store. I'll admit, that was just about as irresponsible, selfish and heartless as she could be. Not only was this woman suffering from extreme cognitive dissonance, but she was common sense deficient too.

It wasn't until later that I conceptualized that her actions in that store were more desperate and trifling than they were intentionally designed to wrong me. Maybe that's just my forgiving heart talking, despite her putting me in harm's way, and the direct negatives that resulted from it. She did what was necessary to undergird her habit. Though her acts were criminal in nature, illegal and immoral, causing physical harm to me or anyone else was not a road she would intentionally travel. Her decisions would land only her in jail, only her under the bridge, only her in the alley, only her in crack houses. Only her. I do recall mom having a few physical encounters though, as she and other addicts squabbled over whatever empty promises they had made to each other, and a few arguments she had with family and friends who refused to give her money. Again, that's not what I would consider a public safety issue. She was defending her repulsive position and that was strictly personal.

Another time, I was sitting on the porch at my aunt's house playing jacks when I noticed mom walking towards me with a limp and what appeared to be a damaged left shoulder. Her walk was completely unbalanced, and her shoulders were in glaring misalignment as one shoulder was raised higher than the other. Her arm movement was restricted, and she was clearly putting more weight on one side. There was a sizable round knot on the back of her head about as big as a golf ball. It was sitting just between the nape of her neck and her left ear. The flesh was slightly open, and I could still see drops of blood peeking through. These were fresh wounds, and they certainly looked like they required some level of physical therapy. I hadn't seen my mom in weeks prior to that moment, and the grief and worry I was experiencing was paralyzing. Who had done this to her? And why? This looked like a vicious attack. And I wanted to know if she was in the clear or if the perpetrator was coming back for round two. I assumed it had something to do with drugs, so going to the hospital probably wasn't an option as that would have invited more legal trouble. She went inside and visited with my aunt for a while, doing her usual, looking for food and asking for a cigarette, and this time aspirin too. They had a conversation from the adjoining rooms, as mom was in the kitchen and my aunt was sitting on the couch in the living room. I could hear questions like, "Where have you been?", "What happened?" and "Are you alright?" That was about all I managed to gain. I didn't go inside that day, I stayed on the porch and continued playing jacks, taking it all in from afar. This wasn't a story I wanted to have a front row seat for. I just wasn't in the mood for whatever drama filled foolishness she was about to spew. About 30 minutes later, she had finished her meal and cigarette, which were the only things she came there for anyway, and slowly made her way out the door where I was sitting. She said, "Bye baby, I'll see you later." I replied, "What happened to you?" She looked at me and said, "Oh you know, I got into it with somebody." That was emphatically clear, but what the hell could have happened for her to be in such bad shape? She could tell in my face that I didn't have room for her lies. No further words were exchanged, and she walked away in undeniable pain and in need of medical care.

It would be years later before I would come to know the truth about her injuries. As the story goes, she attempted to take wax and a white bar of soap and cut it into pieces to simulate crack cocaine. She packaged it up identical to a bag she would purchase on the streets and attempted to sell the fake drugs to a known dealer. Once he discovered the trickery that had taken place, he beat her ferociously with a long metal pipe. She could have died. Her elaborate scheme cost her permanent physical damage. She never walked the same way again. She walked towards me at the Greyhound bus station about ten years later with that same limp. Mom repeatedly put herself in positions like that. Subjecting herself to detrimental results. And no amount of wreckage seemed to be too much. Here we go again, back to her impulsivity and her insatiable need for quick fixes. Boosting stolen baby clothes was a quick fix for money, a quick meal from my aunt, and a quick scheme to sell fake drugs to earn a quick buck. All constructed to offer her immediate results. But she was taking risks of epic size proportions to meet her needs. Risks that were making a durable impact on her life. That was painfully sad. Drugs were going to kill her one way or another. All I could do was pray, and I did often, with my eyes so full of tears that I could hardly see. Wearily hoping that God would save her from herself. My prayer would be, "Dear God, please protect mama. Keep her safe. Take the drugs away. And let her come home, Amen." I was Baptist, but I would finish that prayer with my Catholic school ritual of making the sign of the cross. Followed by blowing a kiss to heaven. That was my way of sealing it, as if those gestures somehow made my prayer reach God faster.

If you've ever seen an addict, one thing is universal: drugs are masterful at tattooing them with permanent physical side effects. Mom was no exception. And as her appearance started to take the shape of a person I couldn't even recognize, I was on my knees that much more. When she stumbled into my sister's apartment, that was the most dreadful I had ever seen her. Her hair was wild, and all over her head. Patches were missing, and she had baldness. It was thin, and gray was coming through. She had no teeth, as the dentures she had adapted to wearing were missing. Her skin was droopy and covered in sores. Her body looked fragile and skeletal. She was the equivalent of a walking corpse. Her arms, hands, legs and even the top of her feet were covered in track marks from the needles she used to shoot up. There were absolutely no patches of smooth or normal looking skin present anywhere. She had permanently damaged the very texture of her skin. It was rough and bumpy and un-aesthetically pleasing to look at. It was outright ugly. Even when she had bouts of sobriety and got cleaned up, her hair would grow, and her face would heal. She would gain weight. But those nasty scars would never go away and would always be the first place my eyes would go.

  I finally got the courage to ask her about those scars. She made up a lie so believable it would have you second guessing yourself. She told me she had been cooking grits and she spilled the hot pot of grits all over herself. I mean her ability to tell lies was Olympic in nature, she deserved a gold medal. I imagine an accident like that could have identical results, because the best way to explain her scars was to put yourself in the mindset of a burn victim. Her skin definitely looked charred. I didn't know if hot grits could produce second or third degree burns or not, but it sounded good. When feeling annoyed or pushed to your limits, there's a common saying, "You're overcooking my grits." Rose was undeniably overcooking my grits with that excuse. I knew better though. I was far smarter than she was giving me credit for. She must have spilled 100 pots of grits to get that many scars. And how would you get grits on the back of your arms and the top of your feet? Even though that was my first time hearing it, assuredly, she had used that excuse a lot. I knew she could see the obvious devastation she was doing to herself. Those scars were daily reminders of a life wasted, so why weren't they enough for her to realize she had much more to live for? Why weren't they enough for her to contemplate all the time she had lost, all the things she didn't get to do? The places she didn't get to go. The school talent shows she missed. The football games I cheered at. The awards ceremonies. My graduations. Her children, grandchildren, sobriety, and health should have had more value than they did. But sorrowfully, they didn't. The only thing she valued was dope.

I haphazardly observed her giving herself one of those scars. Or, should I say, one of those burns from a pot of grits. I was playing outside at my aunt's house, one of those overly spirited games of tetherball. The sun was blistering, and we had been at it for several hours, gulping down water from the nearest hose like camels in a desert, trying to get some relief from the Texas heat. My bladder was full, so I dashed into the house to use the bathroom. I opened the door and saw what I thought was a scene from a horror film. Mom and another junkie were sitting on the bathroom floor getting high. The guy must have overdosed, as his body was limp and unresponsive. She was shaking him and throwing water in his face. A tactic I suspect she had gotten used to performing. I stood there for a few seconds in total terror, with my heart in the pit of my stomach. My stomach was turning about as drastically as it does when going down the steepest peak of a rollercoaster. It was an empty, painful feeling. I gazed at both of them in total dismay. Mom never looked my way or said a word. She was completely engulfed in her role of paramedic, that she was oblivious to my

"She never saw me, I was invisible in that moment."

presence. She never even saw me. I was invisible in that moment. I slammed the door as fast as I could and ran downstairs. Honestly, everything after that horrendous catastrophe was a blur. I can't begin to tell you what I did next. Did I go get someone? Did I call an ambulance? I simply don't remember. I tried to bury that memory deep into the pages of "never happened" land. But that trauma became a permanent imprint in my mind.

From that day forward I hated using that bathroom. All I was ever able to see were the black silhouettes of two lost souls battling the force of death. **Knowing that mom was an addict and seeing the manifestation of its physical effects is one thing, but being a witness to it takes the pain beyond the threshold of tolerance.** What an awful way to live. And why were they so careless about locking the door? Of all the places they could have gone, why did she choose my aunt's house that day? Why would she risk exactly what had just happened? Selfish, irresponsible and impulsive behavior yet again. Mom treated drugs like precious cargo. And that day she was so divorced from reality that she cared more about shooting heroin than she did about being protective of the place of "isolation" she chose to do it in. I'm not positively sure when she and her companion went into the bathroom. I didn't recall seeing anybody go inside. But then again, I was too busy playing tetherball, just trying to be a kid.

Isolated (adjective) - having minimal contact or little in common with others.

Incarcerated (adjective) - the act of being imprisoned or confined.

"Before you can break out of prison, you must realize you are locked up." –Healthy Place

CHAPTER 4
ISOLATED & INCARCERATED

She had come to get me from my aunt's yard where I had been playing and asked me to walk with her to an elderly lady's

apartment in the back of the projects. She was going to visit Ms. Walker, let's just call her that for memory's sake, as I can't remember for the life of me what that sweet lady's name was. She was always interrupting what I was doing to give me a lousy five minutes of her time. I'm not sure what the point really was, we weren't doing anything meaningful, we surely weren't creating any positive memories, only crappy ones, and we weren't bonding over motherly advice, like the do's and don'ts of life or what was happening at school. She didn't need a companion to walk the same repetitiously shameful track she had instituted on a daily basis, that consisted of running in and out of my aunt's house, back and forth to her drug dens and anywhere else she could get a little unworthy mercy from down that same path. Yet, I was always inserted into her rotten sphere for just a "quick minute". To either fill some selfish need or as an attempt to make herself feel better as a mother for at least acknowledging that I was still alive and belonged to her. I think both were true.

We walked through the buildings and across the park in an unknowingly brisk manner until we reached Ms. Walker's apartment. Not uttering a word to each other along the way. Ms. Walker's mobility must have been somewhat limited as the entrance to her apartment was constructed with a wheelchair ramp. We walked up the ramp and discovered Ms. Walker sitting on the porch in a light blue floral housecoat, sporting corn rows and clutching a cane. She possessed a very angelic and gentle presence. She had been sitting outside to grasp some fresh air and enjoy an ice-cold glass of lemonade. As it turns out, sitting outside for a short while every day was the highlight of Ms. Walker's day. She lived alone, and only her neighbor's daughter came by to check on her from time to time to make sure she was eating well and taking her medication. There just wasn't a whole lot of excitement going on for an aging 65+ year old woman with no family around. My mom knew this and found pity from Ms. Walker. I'm sure any kind of company was pleasing to her. Even if it was from a known addict. She craved human interaction just about as much as mom craved getting high. After all, mom was gifted at charming people for her own gain. Ms. Walker was completely blinded that she was being taken advantage of for a consistent place to eat and an inconspicuous hideout from some of the messes Rose caused in "dope alley" and just about every other square inch of the projects. Or maybe she wasn't and just pretended not to see. Mom rushed into the house and told me to have a seat on the couch. After chatting with Ms. Walker for a few minutes, learning all about her love for the game show Wheel of Fortune and fried shrimp, I did just that. I could hear rustling in the kitchen. I sat there for what felt like forever, gazing at the pictures of African American angels on the wall and a coffee table with black figurines on it. Getting restless, I hopped up off the couch and peeked my head into the kitchen. Rose was sitting at that table, spoon and lighter in hand, freebasing crack cocaine. This was obviously scene two from the last horror film I had watched with the bathroom setting. I was mortified. This woman was shameless. I was on the couch and Ms. Walker was outside on the porch. What a recklessly bold move. To say it was irresponsible would be putting it mildly. It was narcissistic in nature. Flagrant. Cavalier. And downright absurd. I stared briefly for a moment in total sadness and ran out of Ms. Walker's apartment all the way back to my aunt's house. I was praying in my head as I ran, the same prayer I always prayed, "Dear God, please protect mama. Keep her safe. Take the drugs away. And let her come home, Amen". That prayer was a constant repeat in my mind. I was still waiting on God to answer it. Because of that chilling experience and others like it, I am perplexed at how addicts reduce their very existence to kitchens, bathrooms, hallways, abandoned buildings, and any other place of isolation that suits their doping needs, for a temporary perception of happiness. And how absolutely nothing else matters. No consequences seemed too Goliath, and my slingshot of hope was no match for her cataclysmic brain feebleness and unwavering thirst. I've heard enough stories to know that most addicts describe the feeling of getting high as, "a rush of good feelings", some even describe it as, "living in a dream" or "being covered by a warm blanket".

Doping itself causes a cycle of isolation, and in relative terms you don't think of happiness and isolation as being friends. But for mom and addicts alike, happiness and isolation gleefully coexisted. Like it did in my aunt's bathroom and in Ms. Walker's kitchen. So, let me get this straight, the theory is, to feel happy, but isolate myself because I'm ashamed of what brings me happiness? Logically, that makes no sense. How can something you often have to lie and steal to get, and hide to use make you so happy? There's a divide between what they do and what they may prefer. They may prefer happiness in the normal sense of what that means, but working towards it poses too difficult a task, so seeking happiness in a temporal, unrealistic sense is preferred. Addicts tell themselves that the happiness they seek can't be achieved through other means, as they are trapped in overwhelming emotions of fear, anger, inadequacy and whatever else handicaps them. **In essence, to understand the mind of an addict, is to know that they live in a place in their heads were cruel words and self-doubt thrive like weeds in a garden.** I understand all of that, and I have empathy. But I will never accept, attaining happiness by way of doping, in a bathroom, or a kitchen, in isolation, as "living".

Those emotions are no different than those felt by just about every human alive at some point or another. What makes one person cave to the pressures of drugs and not another? In Rose's case, genetics, psychological makeup and environmental factors were instrumental, as in the case of most people. Yet, take someone like me, who was subjected to Rose's same genetics, same or partial psychological make-up and pretty much the same drug infested environment, and I never once desired to mask pain or failure with illicit drugs for temporary feelings of happiness. Maybe it was because I hated what drugs had made her become. Maybe it was because I just refused to quit on life. I was born a fighter and that spirit encompassed me, or maybe it just wasn't part of God's divine plan. Honestly, it was probably all of the above. I don't think there will ever be a concrete answer as to why some people become addicts and others don't, but it's pertinent to understand, though taking that first hit is indeed a choice, the person has no control over how the substance interacts with their existing brain chemistry that may lead to abuse and eventually addiction. And we know that addiction is a brain disease. A disease that caused Rose to rob a store, sell fake drugs to a dealer, shoot up in the bathroom, freebase in the kitchen and revive an overdosed friend, all for temporary feelings of happiness that is.

Putting all of that into perspective, those decisions put mom on a carousel in and out of jail and prison. Her unfortunate relationship with law enforcement and the criminal justice system began as early as 1976, when she was just twenty-one years old. Though her drug use had already taken off like a fighter jet years before. She had been arrested more than 63 times and her rap sheet reads like painful, depressing lyrics to a blues song. The lyrics included: criminal trespassing, possession of a controlled substance, theft, unlawful weapon, passing worthless checks, evading arrest, giving fictitious names, cocaine possession and prostitution. I can't fully account for how many times theft and prostitution were duplicated.

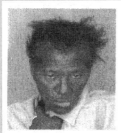

Date: 6/5/2002
Agency: Dallas Police

Date: 10/26/2005
Agency: Dallas County Sheriff

Date: 12/7/2005
Agency: Dallas County Sheriff

They were like the hook to the song; you know the verse you repeat over and over again in between the other verses. Those two had the word "enhanced" by them. "Enhanced" meant she had been arrested on those two charges more than twice before for each one. How much exactly, is still unknown, but they could fill a page of their own. This tells the very grim story of a woman so dependent on a controlled substance that she stole and sold her body to sustain her drug needs. She even resorted to giving fictitious names to avoid being caught.

Partial Arrest Record

1. ROSIE LEE CURLEE - CRIM TRES BLDG AND PROP
2. ROSIE LEE CURLEE - PROSTITUTION
3. ROSIE LEE CURLEE - POSS CONT SUB/3RD
4. ROSIE LEE CURLEE - 12/19/79 PGBC 10 YRS TDC-1/3
5. ROSIE LEE CURLEE - PROST/ENHANCED
6. ROSIE LEE CURLEE - PROSTITUTION
7. ROSIE LEE CURLEE - DWI
8. ROSIE LEE CURLEE - PROSTITUTION
9. ROSIE LEE CURLEE - VIO VIN RESP
10. ROSIE L CURLEE - NO OPS
11. ROSIE L CURLEE - VSRL
12. ROSIE LEE CURLEE - PROSTITUTION
13. ROSIE LEE CURLEE - PROSTITUTION
14. ROSIE LEE CURLEE - PROSTITUTION
15. ROSIE LEE CURLEE - PROSTITUTION
16. ROSIE LEE CURLEE - PROSTITUTION
17. ROSIE LEE CURLEE - PROSTITUTION
18. ROSIE LEE CURLEE - PROS
19. ROSIE LEE CURLEE - T/O 200
20. ROSIE LEE CURLEE - EVADE ARREST
21. ROSIE LEE CURLEE - POSS DANG DRUG
22. ROSIE LEE CURLEE - PROSTITUTION
23. ROSIE LEE CURLEE - POSS CONT SUB/3RD
24. ROSIE LEE CURLEE - MARIHUANA
25. ROSIE LEE CURLEE - PROST
26. ROSIE LEE CURLEE - PWC/THEFT
27. ROSIE LEE CURLEE - PROST/2ND
28. ROSIE LEE CURLEE - DWI
29. ROSIE LEE CURLEE - MARIHUANA
30. ROSIE LEE CURLEE - PROS
31. ROSIE LEE CURLEE - THEFT
32. ROSIE LEE CURLEE - THEFT
33. ROSIE LEE CURLEE - PROSTITUTION
34. ROSIE LEE CURLEE - UNLAWFUL WEAPON
35. ROSIE LEE CURLEE - PROST
36. ROSIE LEE CURLEE - PROSTITUTION
37. ROSIE LEE CURLEE - PROSTITUTION
38. ROSIE CURLEE - VSRL PASS WPLAT
39. ROSIE CURLEE - NO OPS
40. ROSIE CURLEE - NO INS
41. ROSIE CURLEE - FALSE NAME TRAF
42. ROSIE LEE CURLEE - RESIST SEARCH
43. ROSIE LEE CURLEE - PROSTITUTION
44. ROSIE L CURLEE - FICT NAME
45. ROSIE L CURLEE - NO OPS
46. ROSIE L CURLEE - NO INS
47. ROSIE LEE CURLEE - THEFT 20-200
48. ROSIE LEE CURLEE - THEFT 20-200
49. ROSIE LEE CURLEE - EVADE ARREST
50. ROSIE LEE CURLEE - THEFT ENHANCE
51. ROSIE LEE CURLEE - PROSTITUTION
52. ROSIE LEE CURLEE - THEFT ENHAN
53. ROSIE LEE CURLEE - PROSTITUTION
54. ROSIE LEE CURLEE - PROSTITUTION
55. ROSIE LEE CURLEE - PROSTITUTION
56. ROSIE LEE CURLEE - ASLT
57. ROSIE LEE CURLEE - THEFT 20
58. ROSIE LEE CURLEE - PROSTITUTION
59. ROSIE LEE CURLEE - Unspecified Offense
60. ROSIE LEE CURLEE - Unspecified Offense
61. ROSIE LEE CURLEE - Unspecified Offense
62. ROSIE LEE CURLEE - Unspecified Offense
63. ROSIE CURLEE - COCAINE-POSSESS

113

It was not uncommon to see Rose busily moving about the projects with a large duffel bag full of stolen items. That bag was overflowing with tons of bottles of perfume, cartoons of cigarettes and packages of socks and panties. She was the ultimate booster and very experienced at negotiating money in return for whatever items she could manage to sell. I can remember a time when she came to my sister's house and dropped her bag of goodies in the middle of the living room floor. Digging deep into the bottom until she emerged with the perfect bottle of perfume she was trying to gift me. I didn't know how to respond to that gesture of kindness. I understood what she was trying to do, and it was thoughtful, but I wanted no part of anything stolen. It just felt wrong. I intentionally left that perfume at my sister's house. I didn't need or want perfume, I wanted her to get clean and be my mom. Instead, stealing would become her livelihood and jail would become the repetitive consequence.

Speaking of jail, we went to visit my mom once after one of her arrests. Just getting through security cemented in my brain that jail was no place I'd ever want to be. My grandma held my hand as we walked up the steps of the county building. Upon entering the front door, everyone had to put the contents of their pockets in a bucket, send purses or bags through a metal detector and stand with your feet shoulder width apart, and arms outstretched so an officer could frisk you for any prohibited items. I walked ahead of grandma and went through the metal detector first. I had no bags and nothing in my pockets, so I was done in thirty seconds tops. But those thirty seconds seemed like ages since frisking felt so violating. I was just a kid, but that didn't exempt me from the cruelty of the security measures. I watched grandma do the same and gather her belongings before we headed up the elevator. Once we got to the visitors area, grandma and I signed our names as guests to a list and moms name as the inmate.

"I took in the eerie surroundings. Pain, sadness and fear filled my heart."

The guard escorted us to a booth-like space, constricted by two concrete walls, with two chairs and a see-through glass. There was a phone mounted on that concrete wall. While we waited for my mom to emerge from behind the metal door, I took in the eerie surroundings. Pain, sadness and fear filled my heart. The room was engulfed with suffering family members who were shedding tears and some even exchanging laughter at the inmates on the other side of the glass. Hearts were broken, lives were shattered, and freedom felt unattainable. Two scrolls around the room, and it was apparent that I was the only kid there. I suspected this wasn't a place where too many kids frequented very often.

Finally, mom made her way through the metal door

 wearing an all-white inmate uniform. The guard removed the handcuffs from her wrists, and she sat down. She looked well. She was a lot healthier than she had been in recent times. Her face was round from the obvious weight gain, her hair had grown shoulder length and was styled in curls. She was wearing red nail polish and burgundy lipstick. She was beaming with happiness, except

this time it wasn't drug induced. She was genuinely joyful to see me and grandma. Before grandma could blink I had already grabbed that phone. "Hey mom!", I exclaimed. "I'm so happy to see you!" She answered by saying, "Hey baby, I'm happy to see you too. You look so pretty. How's school?" I went on to tell her about winning the school spelling bee, making the cheer team and helping grandma at work from time to time. She told me to keep up the good work, how much she loved me and how she would be out soon. I soaked up her words like a sponge and felt content that she was safe.

Jail isn't a place you would think of for safety, but for me it was an answered prayer that she wasn't on the streets. Going to jail meant she could give her body an essential break from the daily harshness of addiction. She could be sober minded, free in her thoughts and she could enjoy the simple things life had to offer like playing cards, watching TV or reading a book. Since that was about as expansive as things got in jail. She could dream about a better future. About finally being a mom. Grandma graciously took the phone from me and they chatted for a while. I caught pieces of an upcoming court date and needing some money for toiletries and snacks. A short while later we were preparing to leave. Grandma hung up the phone and we waved goodbye and blew kisses through the glass window. We watched as the guard put the handcuffs back on her wrists and listened to the sharp clicking sounds of the bracelets locking as she faded away beyond the metal door. The door making sure to give a resounding BOOM! as it slammed, solidifying the jail's authority over all of us. On our way out, grandma stopped at the commissary and put $20 on mom's books. Incarceration on its face is catastrophic. But I had a love-hate relationship with it. I loved it because it meant she was somewhat safe and healthy, which was something to breathe a little easier about. In like manner I hated it knowing that addiction and crime had led her there, and had taken her away from me, again. Our darkest moments make us who we are, and I had hoped that jail would shine some light on hers. Because of her choices, Rose owed a lot of people apologies. Not just to me, but certainly including me.

> **Daddy's Girl** (noun) - a girl or woman who is particularly attached to, and indulged by, her father.
>
> "The love between a father and daughter knows no distance."
> – unknown

CHAPTER 5
DADDY'S GIRL

Cheer practice had just ended, and I couldn't wait to get home. It was Thursday night which meant Friday would be filled with a pep rally, Texas high school football under the bright lights and spending the night at my cousin's house for the weekend. Dad arrived about five minutes after practice was over and I exhaustedly made my way to the car with my backpack, cheer bag and pom poms in hand. Dad greeted me with, "Hey there kiddo." "Hey daddy", I responded. "You look tired there kid", he said. "I am. But I did pretty good on my math test today", I said in a very fulfilled tone. "That's great, I knew you could do it", daddy said. To know me is to know that I absolutely loathe math. It had been a thorn in my side for just about forever.

119

Numbers weren't my thing. It gave me anxiety. Then you start mixing letters with it like, $x + 6y = 16$ and I'm as lost as Nemo searching for his parents. Daddy knew this and he stayed on me about it. Pushing me daily to my limits to try and get better. He drove about 20 minutes to take me down the 10 minute route to get to my house. He would always ask me what I wanted for

dinner and we would stop by anyplace that sounded appetizing. Sometimes if I needed additional items for school we would swing by the drugstore as well. It was a daily routine we got accustomed to and some nights we skipped the drive thru and opted to dine inside instead. We shared many father-daughter moments across the dinner table. Most of the time we talked about school and all the ball games we had attended. See, daddy worked at a fancy place where all the people had season tickets for every local sports team. We went to all the Cowboys, Mavericks and Rangers games we could endure. I had been going to games since at least the age of five and I knew just about every stat for every player on every one of those teams. I could hold a sports conversation with daddy better than most boys and probably a few men too. Daddy would buy me jerseys and hats for every team in just about every color they made. By the time I met my hubby, daddy had taught me all about football offenses and defenses. I could watch his football games and knew exactly what I was talking about. If he made an interception, that meant he undercut the wide receiver's route and made a quick play on the ball. He was doing his job well by creating that turnover, and I could tease him about not getting there two series prior before that same receiver scored. "Where was that quickness two series ago?" I would say jokingly after the game was over. Daddy taught me all about baseball pitches and jump shots too. I knew that Nolan Ryan was a strikeout machine and batters were dropping like flies at his mean fastball. And Rolando Blackman was making it rain threes. It was pretty cool for a girl to be so well versed on sports. That's a man's world. Isn't it? But that was how daddy and I bonded. After dinner, he would drop me off, head home and be back the very next morning to take me to school. On this particular Friday I reminded him that I was supposed to sleep over at my cousin's house after my football game. He firmly stated, "If your grades aren't right, you're not staying anywhere." As a cheerleader we had weekly grade checks for our coach and that meant daddy too. He was a disciplinarian who put lots of emphasis on the importance of grades and I worked hard to make sure I was flexing my academic muscle and living up to expectations.

Daddy was a very intellectual man who had lots of academic successes and professional achievements of his own. After graduating from high school, he attended college on a golf scholarship and later earned a Bachelor's degree in History. He then served four years in the United States Army before going back to school to earn a Master's degree in Family Guidance Counseling. Daddy was smart, professional and one of the most deliberate people I knew. He was assertive, driven and highly productive. I admired his meticulous stewardship and tried to mimic myself after his example. If there ever was a role model, daddy was it. They say opposites attract, but I've never seen two more vastly different people than mom and dad. A high school dropout and a two-time degree holder. This was the perfect manifestation of God's sense of humor.

Due to my mom's addiction and absence, dad found himself overcompensating for her failures. Daddy drove 40 minutes a day to pick me up for school and from cheer practice, attended all my games, made trips to Sam's to buy food for the week, shopped for clothes, including bras and even feminine hygiene products. I'm glad he was there to provide for me, but I would turn as red as Rudolph's nose walking down the aisle to pick out maxi pads and pimple cream. This was the type of stuff that most moms would handle. Most sober moms, that is. But the one thing I loved most about him was his giving heart. Nobody could beat daddy giving, I mean nobody. Every Friday in elementary and middle school he would give me and Tonya allowance money, and he would give away sports tickets like a game show host dishing out prizes. He also gave large sums of spending money to anyone who dared to invite me someplace or allowed me to spend the night, whether we had plans to go anywhere or not, and he would give away whole turkeys, hams, and steaks to anyone who would cook it. Those were expensive food items. He even gave to people he had no obligation to just because he was being nice. It's who he was.

I was protective of my daddy, and I found myself infuriated sometimes by his generosity. People would see him coming and would hold their hands out like panhandlers on the street asking for money. More times than not, he would oblige too. He was like Santa Claus when he came to the projects. I'd be so mad that I'd turn into Mike Tyson, throwing uppercuts, left hooks and right jabs in the air. These same people would have the worst things to say about him when he didn't fulfill their selfish desires and passed on giving them money, that was rare, but it happened occasionally. It showed me what people really valued, and I was hostile at the thought of them taking advantage of him. But daddy wasn't fooled. He was fully aware of exactly how they felt about him and what they would say behind his back. It didn't matter though, he was just a giver to his core. He still is. His character and heart are unmatched. People could say stuff about my mom, and it would undeniably hurt me in my soul, but say something about my daddy and I was ready to fight. I'll never forget some of those comments. They were vile and completely undeserving. He was just the man that gave them $20, but to me he was my hero. The Most Valuable Player in my life.

Christmases were more of the same. He would show up

early before I could change my pajamas with a huge bag draped over his shoulder. It was full of presents for me. He even made multiple trips to his car to get more gifts, it was like

he was running back and forth to his sleigh. Weeks earlier I had given daddy a "wish list" and just about everything on that list was in that huge bag. Those are memories that I will treasure forever. I can just see him walking around the mall looking for a pink jacket, a lip gloss kit and gold earrings. One year I even asked for a Michael Jackson leather jacket and the famous white glove. It was the hottest item of the season. They were sold out everywhere. I'm not quite sure how he pulled it off, and say what you will about MJ, but I was the coolest kid around that year. As much as daddy was a giver, he was just as much a teacher. He was no nonsense in his approach, and I think the orderliness of military life paired with the bitterness of mom's addiction put him keenly on a path to give me both cultural and social balance and greater economic and educational opportunities. I don't doubt for a second that he was doing everything humanly conceivable to stop me from being like Rose. It was pretty apparent. From private schools to ice skating lessons to playing in the band, SAT prep classes and fancy parties with esteemed people from his job. I was the only kid in the projects who wore uniforms and carried ice skates and a clarinet in my bag. You name it, daddy encouraged it and I tried it. He never said a word, other than "How much do I owe?" That became his battle cry for undergirding all of my interests.

I may have missed out on a lot of nurturing from my mom, but daddy made up the difference. All along the way, he was teaching me not to be a victim of my circumstances. He instilled considerable character traits in me while simultaneously exposing me to greater capabilities. It was a life accomplishment of the largest proportion when kids in the projects graduated from high school and it was especially commending if they managed to do it without getting pregnant or going to jail. They weren't making plans for college, but were entering the workforce at an early age, making the minimum wage and doing jobs that didn't require much intellect or skill. Private school provided me with no guarantees for a better shot at going to college, but it sure set me on the path and equipped me with all the right tools to get there. My job was to take the knowledge they offered and apply it. Daddy came from a family where just about everyone went to college. The likes of Harvard and Stanford, to name a few. College was not a casual option I entertained, rather a certainty and a question of where. Ice skating lessons and SAT classes were cultural and social experiences too. I was the only black girl in both. I was terrible at ice skating, but you couldn't tell me that I wasn't going to be the next Debbie Thomas. I may not have been good at it, but it was the exposure I was gaining. The ability to see and partake in things not typically attainable to kids like me. In the SAT classes I excelled at the writing portion, that was my comfort zone. I cruised through it like an ice cream truck on a hot summer day. Nice and easy. Math, that was another story. I was just average. I learned a thing or two, but thank goodness the writing portion could carry me over the finish line. I told you, numbers and letters just don't belong together. Daddy saw the long-term profit in all of it. **And allowing me to see the other**

side of the world was vitally as important as protecting me from the one I was in. Those character traits he was trying to instill, they came effortlessly. I can see how daddy used my weakness in math and my consciousness about my mom to drive home the gravity of learning to push myself to greater limits, not to make excuses, to be responsible for my actions, and to create my own possibilities. He was busy "not making excuses" either. He never complained about all the running around my schedule required or the amount of money it was going to cost. He just did it. I was fervently complaining about those SAT classes and he never once mentioned being one of the only dads at parent teacher conferences or my high school football games. Daddy loved football, so I figured being at the games wasn't too bad, but most of my cheer squad teammates were accompanied by their moms or both parents if they were married. Telling people that my dad was the lone parent because my mom was an addict was not a revelation I wanted to broadcast. Those close to me knew. But for the most part, it was a secret never to be told. There was never a Friday night when I was cheering that I couldn't look up and see daddy sitting in those stands, wearing school colors and clapping for me. He was doing some cheering too.

We had a lot of stuff to cheer about together. Placing second in the science fair, winning the school spelling bee, playing goalie for my soccer team and getting recognized for academic performance on state issued tests. We also cheered about being inducted into the National Honor Society, getting accepted into college, making the collegiate cheer team and joining my sorority. And much more. Daddy was there through it all. He made it all possible. He bought every science ingredient, bought every book, paid for every application, uniform and membership fee. And he did it with no complaints. He even consoled me when I didn't make the volleyball team, when I broke my finger and my ankle, and when I got my first speeding ticket. A few of those things warranted screams of, "What were you doing?" and "Why were you driving so fast?" I guess I deserved that. It had just cost him additional medical bills and traffic fines.

By the time I started college he was starting to give me more personal freedom to grow. I hadn't realized it though and I was still deathly afraid to disappoint him. I can remember wanting to change my major and contemplating just how I was going to manage pulling it off. My entire high school career had been filled with taking computer classes, since I was in the computer cluster. I took one programming class and quickly realized that it just wasn't a fit for me. It was worse than math! There was an infinite amount of entries that made no sense.

There were more letter and number combinations and I felt like I was learning another language that I would never learn to speak. I couldn't get to the registrar's office fast enough. I prepared myself for the worst, then I told him. Pleasantly, he was accepting of my decision. He had been in college before and he knew that dropping classes was all a part of the process. I had worried my little self for nothing. But I was only beginning to see how daddy would let me fly on my own. Soon after that, he handed me a credit card with my name on it. My only instruction was to let him know if I purchased anything over a $100. I thought I was doing big stuff, I no longer had to ask for money, but he was trusting me to spend whatever I wanted. Within reason of course. I never bought much except gas and food but knowing that he trusted me was soothing.

Speaking of trust, a short time later he came down to watch one of our home basketball games. This would be the day that I was going to introduce my boyfriend to him. My boyfriend was a handsome guy, who played on the football team and possessed a certain level of personal character. He wore jeans, polo style shirts, hiking boots and earrings. The minute I met him I knew those earrings were going to be a problem. I grabbed

my pom poms and walked toward the bleachers to meet my dad.

Because sports bonded us, he went on to tell me all about the

shots we missed, the lazy defense that was played and the bad

clock management. You would have thought we had lost and not

just won by eight. Dad was an avid golfer and somewhat of an

athlete himself, so missed opportunities didn't sit well with him.

I spotted my boyfriend from across the gym floor and signaled

for him to come over. He walked up, introduced himself and

shook daddy's hand. I kid you not, the first thing out of daddy's

mouth was, "What are you doing with those earrings on?" "I

don't trust a man who wears earrings." I was completely

humiliated and my eyes were as big as balled fists. There was

nothing left to do but shake my head with agitation. After talking

for a minute and realizing that he was the star defensive player

for the football team and had a real chance of going pro, that

whole not trusting a man with earrings thing, went right out the

window. Football was the way to daddy's heart. At least it was

that day. Six months later, my boyfriend did go pro, and it was

like winning the lottery for daddy since he went to his favorite team. When I told daddy the great news, his predictable response was, "How 'bout them Cowboys!" This man went from lecturing my boyfriend about earrings to wearing his jersey to the games. It was glorious! It was truly disheartening that mom never made it to a single one of those games. But you could count on daddy being there, just like he was when I looked into the stands on Friday nights. It didn't take my boyfriend long to figure out that my daddy was my world, and if I was ever going to learn to trust him, he had better be at least half the man my daddy was. I had no vacancies left for any more disappointments. Fortunately for me, things went well for daddy and my new boyfriend. They started having their own sports conversations that didn't include me. Wasn't I the glue that bonded these two together? And wasn't sports the one thing we all had in common? I'm being childishly asinine, because I was geeked at their respect for each other and their ability to enjoy each other's company. They would go on forever talking about good players, bad players, and everyone in between. It was like watching *Sanford & Son* decide on which pieces to keep in the junkyard. I can't conclusively say how mom and dad ever came to be, and honestly it really doesn't matter much. But I'm certain that daddy was blindsided by mom's addiction. Early on she was a highly functioning addict. And apparently a mighty fine actress too. She gave him more headaches than Tylenol had pills, but he never displayed any anger or frustration to me. I got the same loving and giving daddy all the time. The Friday night

game daddy. The pink jacket buying daddy. The sports nut daddy. It served me well, as I needed his sensible balance over her eradication. Mom made an infinite amount of mistakes. But one of the greatest things she ever did was choose the absolute best daddy for me. Daddy is unmistakably in a league of his own. A true MVP.

Chain Breaker (noun) - a person that breaks the chains they have seemingly been **held down** by. Not falling into the **statistics**. Making it out of poverty and other dysfunctional realities.

"You were not created to be bound: bound by loneliness, by shame. Our God is a chain breaker. This is a new day. Freedom is coming." – unknown

CHAPTER 6
<u>Chain Breaker</u>

I can't name a single thing in the world scarier than becoming a parent. The task of being responsible for another

human life is pretty substantial. On January 9, 2002, parenting became a reality for me. Born to me was a six pound, thirteen ounce beautiful baby girl. I can recall how excited I

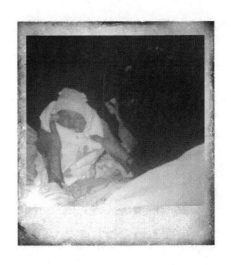

was throughout my entire pregnancy and how I took intricate

care of myself to provide my baby with the best start I could give her. Her complete and total well-being was on me. I read as many books as I could put my hands on, I placed headphones on my belly so she could hear music, and I was very cautious of everything I digested into my body and hers. From prenatal vitamins and food to liquids and medicine. The scrutiny of everything was done with her in mind. I was a huge fan of coffee and started every day with a cup of hot joe, and though coffee is ok in pregnancy as long as the intake is moderate, I let that go too. We took lamaze classes, frequent walks and I even participated in jazzercise until my sixth month. I didn't wear high heels because of the risk of falling and I stopped coloring my hair. I pretty much sacrificed everything to make sure the life I was creating was safe. Most mothers can relate to some or all of these selfless deeds. But when I read the pages of Rose's criminal past, the only thing that mattered to her was herself. Even during pregnancy.

In the margins of those pages were piles of arrests during the months in which she was carrying me. As much time as she spent in jail, I'm pleasantly dumbfounded that I wasn't actually born there. Addiction on its face is selfish, and even in pregnancy her cravings for drugs diluted any motherly instincts or desire to do what was necessary for her unborn child. She completely ignored that inner voice that said, "What about the baby?" Her brain disease appeared to be blazing out of control, without a single drop of water close by to put the fire out. She was running rampant in the streets and even her frequent visits to jail weren't offering much relief, since most of the charges were misdemeanors. She could sit that out in a few days and be right back at it. No pregnancy was going to derail her habit. And it didn't. I came from this woman, but we were so mightily different that its mind boggling. I knew the moment I found out that I was having a girl that God was giving me this gift to allow me to be the mother to her that I never had. A mom that would comb her hair, paint her nails, have pretend tea parties and read her stories. A mom who would walk her to kindergarten, buy her first pair of soccer cleats and play in makeup. We did all of that.

Being pregnant alone changed my perception of the world, and every decision that followed came with this little person in mind. But that's never the reality of a child born to an addict. And it unquestionably wasn't mine. **Children born to addicts are afterthoughts over drugs and are already at a disadvantage. In some part, before they even take their first breath, their life's stories are already written. An undesirable birthright gives them exclusive membership to a club that nobody wants to be a part of. Their susceptibility to addiction is considerably increased, some may have to be administered drugs as a way of weaning them off and reducing withdrawal symptoms, and severe emotional, mental and physical barriers are likely truths. It's categorically unfair**. It was nothing short of a miracle that I had no significant mental or physical side effects, because as you know, I too was a dopesick newborn, who entered this world with heroin and cocaine flowing through my veins, who was administered weaning medications, and battled with undeserving withdrawals of my own for the first week of life. I thank God for covering me in her womb, as venomous of a place as it was, I recognize His power to protect me and allow me to become a chain breaker. For me, disadvantage came in the form of emotional fragility. I functioned in a constant emotional state of both pity and total anger. I had so much sadness for what mom had authorized herself to become. For the lack of courage she displayed in allowing her drug use and the "temporary happiness" it provided to determine her character. Her absence of fight for herself had become total surrender to the power of drugs. It was a helpless and discouraging thing for me to see. This was pity. Then there was the relentless anger that festered like a volcano waiting to erupt. There were continuous feelings of neglect, abandonment and disregard. Even rage. This was anger. And it would rear its ugly head through my flippant yet hostile attitude and derogatory mouth. The constant disappointment of Rose not taking advantage of her occasional sobriety to at least attempt to repair the damage she had caused me, factored into my distrust of people, my selfishness and instincts to retaliate against hurt with hurt.

There were times when kids would tease me for "looking like a white girl," and since that insult alone didn't move me, the assured way to get under my skin would be to seal the deal with visceral meanness like, "Hey white girl, that's why your mama is a crackhead." Instead of ignoring them or finding someone else to play with, I would turn into a fire breathing dragon, hurling belittling comments of my own like, "Your mama is with mine and they smoking together!" and "That's why you don't have a daddy and your mama is on welfare!" Wow! Those words were merciless. They definitely weren't the ideal thing to say. Especially since welfare and minimum wage jobs were how people stayed afloat in the projects. In fact, it was just the opposite of what daddy was telling me to do. But daddy didn't have to deal with those kids everyday. In all honesty, it felt good to hurt them like they hurt me, even if it was momentary. As I said before, I wasn't much of a fighter and I didn't have to be, because my mouth paid dividends. I would make continuous other vulgar comments like that and the kids would eventually leave me alone. But I'm certain that my mom's condition, and the fact that the entire projects knew about it, was what put me on edge, with my boxing gloves on, ready for a prize fight. I couldn't hurt Rose for the pain she caused, but getting back at those kids felt like pure triumph. Any bullying, childish disagreement or feeling of unfairness always resulted in talking about somebody's mama. I was sensitive about my mom and embarrassed by her, but I defended her at all costs, and nobody was going to engage in a verbal war with me that I didn't win. It's fair to say that I had verbal wars just about everyday. I was always victorious though, as I had more ammunition than those kids did, but it never once stopped them from attacking me. When I became a new mom myself to my precious baby girl, I vowed so many times to always be present and available for her. She would never experience the heaviness of not feeling loved, important or neglected. I would show daily confirmations of such and she would become one of the most important people in my life. And she would know it. She wasn't going to have to fight any verbal wars. I was breaking that chain.

As a kid still living in the hood, I spent a substantial amount of time setting my sights on greater things. Allowing my imagination to take me to a fantasy world where life's inadequacies didn't exist and I could create my own happy endings. Time after time I would raid grandma's closet and dress up in high heels and a blazer from one of her suits. Even borrowing her best wig and Fashion Fair fuchsia lipstick. I would grab an oversized hand held bag and stuff it with newspapers and old magazines, those were my important documents. Aggressively, I would bust through the door of my room as if entering a court of law, and I would throw the bag on the dresser and say, "Your Honor, I am Attorney Kim and I am here to represent my client Rose." I would pull the newspapers out of the bag and say, "I'd like to enter into evidence these documents that prove my client is innocent." Arms folded I paced back and forth in my room, walking from one side of the bed to the other as if impatiently waiting for the judge to answer. Then in a deep voice, I would say under my breath, "Attorney Kim, you have proven your case and your client Rose is free to go." It was a whole scene I acted out by myself. And for quite a while, I wanted to be a real life attorney so I could help my mom. I have no recollection of just how many times I acted out that scene, but it was considerable. One of my true talents as a kid was turning tragic moments and fears into something I could manage. If only those walls could talk, I would have a well-written script for a Lifetime movie.

Mom wasn't the only person around me who had a drug problem, and in my mind, I was the attorney who saved everybody. The thought that drugs were becoming a familial epidemic was dire. I can't tell you how many times I peed in a cup to help one person or another transport the virgin urine to the parole office, work or a similar place to beat the system and pass mandatory drug tests. A few were experimenting with the hard stuff, but it was mostly marijuana they were trying to hide, and I played a pivotal role in it. As a result, **I was hellbent on breaking the cycle of addiction.** Every life decision I made was strategically designed to guarantee just that and would carry me away from drugs and the impoverished mediocrity of Pleasant Grove and the projects. After my first year of college, I came home for the summer. Being there felt restraining and unproductive. I had just spent the previous nine months on a collegiate campus where knowledge and learning were preeminent, where careers were being born and dreams were being fulfilled. Where everyone was making plans for the future. Books were my new accessory and the library was the new hang out. Home felt dark. I was back to hearing gunshots ring out, police and ambulance sirens and seeing drug dealers in the pathways of the apartment buildings. Every girl my age was pregnant, and the guys were walking around with their pants so low you could see every inch of their underwear. It felt like stepping in quicksand. A sinking of sorts. Everything was stagnant and nobody was moving anywhere. The force of "barely getting by" was literally weighing me down. There was complacency with working a minimum wage job with no possibility of growth and no medical or retirement benefits for life down the road. I knew I no longer belonged there.

I had dreams of living in a new city with less crime. Of owning a home in a neighborhood with nice trees, on a street that I wasn't afraid to walk down and of taking fancy vacations. Even buying stock. It's how the white kids I used to go to school with lived, and it was exactly the lifestyle of the affluent family my grandmother was still nannying for. A degree was going to help get me there so I could market myself well enough to make the big bucks. The chain of not "dreaming bigger" was being broken too. I never came home another summer, I stayed in summer school and pressed my way through, semester after semester until my goal was complete. Four years later, a graduate and married, my hubby and I took our first fancy

144

vacation, a honeymoon to Hawaii and afterwards reported to the New Orleans Saints for his new job. I got both my vacation and my new city! We lived in the suburbs on the outskirts of town where there was less crime, on a very long street where you drove through a huge tunnel of well-manicured trees! I dared to dream, and God answered.

A chain in a tangible sense is a metal object of great strength used for confining. But in a figurative sense, it's a mindset or emotion that blocks or stifles our mental growth and well-being. Every Mother's Day I wrestle with the emotional chain of guilt. Outside of Christmas, it's one of the most celebrated holidays in our current social climate. And rightfully so. I mean, who doesn't love their mom? Doesn't everybody have the perfect representative of selflessness? Our moms are directly responsible for the people we become and the influence we have on society. For how we treat others and handle conflict. Moms are sacrificial lambs for the stability, growth and welfare of the lives they create. And we turn into raging lions when anything threatens to harm our kids. I wish I knew what that felt like. Not once did I spend a single Mother's Day with Rose, celebrating her for giving me life, for the years of uninterrupted atonement of packing my lunch, washing my cheer uniform or working on class projects. For calming my fears of a monster being under my bed or encouraging me to do something I was insecure about. For wiping my tears or kissing my boo boos. There were no fancy brunches, no flowers or cards to give. Mother's Day leaves me emotionless and numb. Incapable of warm fuzzy feelings of love and gratefulness. Instead, I feel guilty for not having more cheerful emotions towards her. The societal cliché "you can't miss what you didn't have" angers me. I absolutely missed a normal, functional mother-daughter relationship with Rose. And until I realized that Santa Claus was a childhood fictional character, bringing her home was always at the top of my wish list. Contrarily, the chain of being emotionless subsides as my hubby and three children go to overwhelming lengths to make Mother's Day extra special for me. Complete with brunch or dinner at any restaurant of my choice, and a shower of flowers, cards and other gifts. And all the hugs and kisses I can handle. If I was lucky, I'd get a handmade coupon book to use at my leisure for tasks like taking out the trash and putting away the dishes. Those were the cutest sentiments of their attempts to take some pressure off of me. My favorites are the self-drawn pictures of their little handprints. Inscribed with three words, "Happy Mother's Day". Those simple pieces of art make my heart melt, because a mother holds her child's hand for a little while, but their heart forever.

Rose struggled ever so mightily to break all of her chains. They always kept her from celebrating anything. At least with me they did. Mother's Day and birthdays would come and pass without even the slightest

acknowledgement. In much the same way as cars speeding by on a highway. One after another, in accelerated continuity. This

147

further demonstrates the stronghold that drugs have, as nobody in their right mind would choose that life. A life with no celebrations, no meaningful relationships and no sense of accomplishment. But of purposeful and calculated danger. I know in my soul that in some part Rose had these struggles because she relied on her own strength. I didn't know her to be a godly person, even in the moderate sense. I'm positive she knew God, but I'm not convinced she had a real relationship with Him. There's a proven difference based off results. But as a Christian myself, I know that I have to trust God in my times of trouble. Philippians 4:13 tells us that, we can do all things through Christ who gives us strength. Maybe she should have given God a better try and relied on His strength. She spent a lot of time running from her past and trying to make sense of it. Nothing worked, and I recognize that there are no simple fixes for her complex problems. But nothing is too hard for God. If you take one step towards Him, He'll take several steps towards you. Whether she realized it or not, God was definitely the one keeping her alive with all the harm she was causing herself. And I know it was Him who protected me in her womb. I whimper at what possible outcomes could have been had faith played a larger role. Ultimately, God gives us free will though. The freedom to choose Him. The freedom to choose drugs. And the freedom to know the difference.

Free will is our ability to act at our own discretion. It's the moral tug of war between what's right and wrong. What we should do versus what we want to do. Unsurprisingly, she always chose the latter. Breaking the chain of self-pity was a task for me too. I swear this woman would come up with more pitiful excuses than a kid who didn't do their homework, as a means to justify her actions and the guilt that rarely came with it. Every now and then while paying an occasional visit to my grandma, I would randomly spot her on the street. I'd find a place to park the car, reach my head out the window and yell, "Hey!" or "Hey Rose!" until she could hear me. I would be far too embarrassed to call her mom, for myself and for the sake of whomever was around. What kind of daughter would I look like? Yelling from a luxury car to an obvious addict I was referring to as mom. She would walk up to my car for just a few minutes, long enough for me to ask, "Where have you been?

When was the last time you ate? and Why haven't you tried to call me?" She would give the same predictable and pathetic response, "Baby, I lost your number." There's no sufficient rebuttal to something so outlandish other than to just say "Ok", nod in agreement and give her the number again. The same number that had been in place for years, the same number she could have gotten from my sister or aunt, the same damn number she used to contact me when she was about to be released from prison. Yeah, that number! Rose never really cared about seeing me. There were no questions of, how are you doing? or how's my granddaughter? She only walked up to that car to entertain me long enough for her to ask that dreaded question, "Hey daughter, you got any spare change or a couple of dollars I can have?" The answer was always, "No. But I can buy you something to eat." Most of the time she would get profoundly frustrated and yell, "I don't want no food!" And start walking off with mumbles of, "Alright, I'll see you later then", with her back turning to me and throwing her hands up in disgust. She had her nerve! How was she mad at me? I know she was desperate, but sheesh! I had a tractor trailer full of reasons to be mad. There was no way I was going to give her any money and take my place as a co-author of the death story she was writing. But if things were really bad, she would take a McDonald's value meal instead. And that $5 meal would probably be the best thing she had eaten in days. I couldn't buy into Rose's pity pitfalls, but make sure that I was breaking that chain too so it wouldn't become a crutch later in life for not taking responsibility for myself. If I had followed her lead, I would have had a black belt at inducing self-pity to earn favorable sympathy or physical, tangible gains from people. I've swallowed a few sour grapes, and each situation provided its own set of opportunities to manipulate people through self-pity. Let's call it what it is: manipulation. A false state or exaggeration of actual existence. Let's start with the monstrous thunderstorm of 2003.

We had just listed our house on the market and within three weeks we had three families come back for multiple showings. One family was even about to submit an offer. At four months pregnant with my second child, I packed my then one year old in the car and headed out to run errands so the impressed family could see the property again. I found myself at the nail salon, with a baby, picture books and a stuffed Elmo doll on my lap. While sitting there, I received a phone call from my realtor. She told me to hurry home because my house had just been struck by lightning and she would meet me there. I frantically packed my daughter up, leaving behind the books and Elmo and rushed home as fast as I could. When I got to the entrance of my subdivision, the police were blocking the streets to not allow any additional traffic through. I was forced to roll down my window and yell at the officer, "That's my house that's on fire!" He moved the barricade and allowed me to enter. I drove up to what appeared to be a live scene from the 1991 film, *Backdraft*.

The fire was blazing forcefully; Thank God it was contained to mostly the upper floor. The fire department caused substantial damage of their own by tearing out the ceiling in the kitchen so that the water that was falling from upstairs would have a place to escape. Otherwise, the results would be the same as the ceiling would eventually collapse from the pressure. The water was several inches high downstairs and all the flooring was ruined and had to be replaced. The rebuilding process would take a year and we would have to move someplace temporarily for the time being. I was pregnant with a small child and alone when that tragedy happened, as my husband was at work, participating in the Atlanta Falcons training camp. I could have kicked self-pity into overdrive and used that experience to get people to buy into a helpless pregnant lady narrative. Using pity to my advantage to get people to feel sorry for me and take any offers of help, food or babysitting whether I needed it or not. That's not who I was, and it was definitely not what I did. But it was indeed who I watched Rose become. In fact, she had done it to Ms. Walker a myriad of times. The thought never even entered my mind.

Watching Rose play that card all those years gave me the mental strength to break that chain with the force of a wrecking ball. I would never allow such an unflattering portrait of myself to be painted and by pure virtue alone, my moral compass wouldn't allow it either. She was of the mindset that she couldn't call me because she didn't have the number, nor a phone or a place to call from. And she wanted me to accept those answers as sorrowful facts. They were truths, but all self-induced ones. I didn't offer her the pity she was seeking because she managed to call when in her mind, the stakes were considerably higher. Accepting her pitiful excuses meant condoning her dismal behavior. It would be allowing her to drift further away from the truth and her continual escape from responsibility. I didn't pity why she couldn't call me, even though that's what she was gambling on. I deeply pitied how she allowed herself to be in that place to begin with. Why wasn't asking your daughter for drug money a moment so humbling that all hustling and selfishness ceased to exist? If only for that moment, why wasn't shame an emotion that she appeared to possess? Just like everything else, the consciousness of her foolish behavior never gave her discomfort. Or maybe it did. But it sure wasn't visible. That in itself was troubling, because it was symptomatic of just how far she had fallen. There were no lines drawn in the sand that she wouldn't cross, and I think she was one "really" bad day away from losing her life, as she always seemed to be standing on the doorstep of disaster. **As much as I'd like to pat myself on the back for breaking the chains of verbal wars, addiction, not dreaming bigger and self-pity, I am yet to be**

154

freed from the emotional chain of guilt. Throughout this journey, you've probably noticed that I sometimes refer to her as mom, and other times she's just Rose. That's essentially because she was two different people in my eyes. In tender moments of hope and the childhood innocence of making wishes, she was the mom I longed to be close to and reserved a special place in my heart for. I eagerly anticipated the day that she would choose me over drugs and the days of making up for lost time would begin. Rose was the selfish person who cared only about the next high, who put me in dangerous situations and led a life of crime. She was the person that I would never be able to save. The little girl in me wanted greatly for mom to make adult decisions and do her job to try and protect me. For her to shield me from the daily hardship of what having a relationship with her was like. To at least pretend that she had my best interest at heart. Every time, she would let me

> "In those moments, she no longer felt like mom, she was just Rose."

down and abandon her responsibility to me. In those moments

she no longer felt like mom, she was just Rose. Knowing this, I carry daily guilt for not being more emotionally connected to her. As the fetus in her womb, we were connected by the umbilical cord of life. The flexible human structure made of blood vessels that served as a transportation unit. I took into my body everything she took into hers. We shared the same blood. I could hear her heartbeat and feel her emotions. Yet, outside of her womb, I couldn't even force emotional connectivity. It was as structurally impossible as trying to fit a square peg into a round hole or searching for satellite service in the desert. The mental dimensions and capacity just didn't exist. There were no joys outside of being released from jail and no victories other than the ones that came from skipping past the bridge and alley. But what did woefully exist were the apparent reverse roles we had taken on. I was indeed the more mature one in the relationship and the authoritative voice that frequently found myself offering childish rebukes of, "You need to leave that stuff alone" and pleas of "Mama please stop, get some help." All which seemingly fell on deaf ears. I was a child who was screaming on the inside that she would honor one of those vacant promises she would make while still being locked up in jail. The same promise of "I'm staying clean this time. You don't have to worry about that." A promise that was yet to come to pass, as she was once again a victim of the repetitious deadly cycle of addiction she had created for herself. Her words offered no value. **I guess where you stand is often determined by where you sit.**

Side Effect (noun) - a secondary, typically undesirable effect of a drug or medical treatment.

"Addiction: the disease that makes you too selfish to see the havoc you created, or care about the people whose lives you have shattered." - Ocean Recovery Center

CHAPTER 7
NASTY SIDE EFFECTS

"Mrs. Mathis the baby is absolutely beautiful. She's healthy and all of her vitals look great. I'll be back shortly to administer her immunizations", said nurse Jane. "Ok, thank you nurse", I gladly responded. Nurse Jane walked out of the door and I slowly rocked my new baby as she rested peacefully in my arms. About ten minutes later, nurse Jane re-entered the room with a clipboard in one hand and a small metal tray with two needles on it in the other. "You can lay her down right here, Mrs. Mathis", she stated. I slowly got up from my seat and took three steps toward the table to lay my baby down. I stepped aside and watched as the nurse removed the cap from the first needle, and without as much of a pinch to grab any fatty tissue, nurse Jane stabbed my baby girl in her thigh, about as quickly as a hand jerks away from touching a hot stove. I mean it looked like a violent stab and it was lightning quick. There was no gentleness, which in my mind such a task required. And before I could blink, a second stab to the other thigh. My baby wailed in pain. She cried so hard that her eyes were pinned shut and her mouth was wide open and literally no sound was coming out. I was pissed and mad as hell! Why did she have to stab her so hard? And so fast? Where was the sympathy? The tenderness? She was only eight weeks old and all of eleven to thirteen pounds. "You guys are all done. Take the band-aids off in about an hour", nurse Jane said. I had no response, as the only thing I could manage to give was a vicious look and a head nod of "ok", as I walked back and forth around the room, bouncing my baby, desperately trying to get her to stop crying.

That experience did nothing but maximize my perception that needles suck! And that day nurse Jane sucked too, but needles do nothing except cause pain. That needle caused my baby pain, it caused Rose a lifetime of pain and as a residual side effect, it caused me pain. I've always been fearful

of needles and I was not the model patient myself when it came

time for shots. As a teenager in high school, I remember having

to get my final booster shot. The moment my daddy told me my

anxiety went from bearable to debilitating. Total fear captivated

me. I hated shots more than anything. Going to the dentist would

have been a better option. For the next few days I did nothing

but labor over how painful it was going to be. I remembered the

last one, and it hurt so bad that I promised myself I would

pretend to be sick to avoid doing that again. Finally, the day had

come. Daddy and I took our place in the designated chairs and

waited for the nurse's instructions. She made a series of

disclaimers, but I didn't hear a thing, I was completely blocking

her out trying to mentally prepare myself. The nurse asked me

my birth date, but her voice seemed to go mute and daddy tapped

me on the leg to hurry and answer. She grabbed an alcohol swab

and rubbed it in an area on the side of my shoulder and quickly

jabbed me with the needle. "Ow!", I screamed as I started to jerk

away. That hurt as bad as I had remembered. "You're all done",

she said while unwrapping a band-aid. I grabbed my arm and

started rubbing it and hurriedly made my way to the door. I left daddy to wrap up with the nurse on his own. I couldn't get to the car fast enough. My arm hurt for at least three days after that and it was incredibly sore. I got yelled at in cheer practice because I was struggling to lift my arms up. As painful as that one experience was, I just couldn't understand why Rose was purposely doing that to herself on a daily basis. Sometimes but not always, consciously tying anything she could find on her arm, a shoelace, rubber band or something similar, using her teeth and free hand to make the dreaded knot, in a hopeful attempt to find a vein and penetrate it with the syringe filled poison elixir. She was literally inflicting pain to escape pain.

That didn't seem like a fair tradeoff. But it was the daily reward that she sought. Then after seeing Rose and her friend shoot up in my aunt's bathroom, and the danger and near death it caused, my fear morphed into total phobia. Thank heaven I'm past the age of needing mandatory shots, because I can't even stomach to get a flu shot. Even the occasional blood work still makes me cringe. Nurse Jane and no one else on the pediatrician's staff would have to worry about me giving them the look of death ever again, as I vowed to never enter the room and watch a child of mine receive immunizations. That trend still stands to this day. I have three kids and they all require their own immunization schedule, so you do the math. In my baby's case, the needle was used to give essential medicine designed to guard her body against infection and disease, a lot like a protective shield. For Rose, the needle was used to provide a falsified sense of reality and allowed her to escape from her actual existence. A kind of numbness. It had just the opposite effect of the meds given to the baby, and was causing irreversible damage, both internally to her organs and externally, to her arms, legs and anyplace she could find to inject one.

For me, I watched the needle take my mom away. Piece by piece as if peeling back the layers of an onion until there was nothing left. Not only did the needle offer her empty, worthless ends, but it also caused her severe medical issues and she contracted Hepatitis C as a risky result. Hepatitis C is a blood-borne virus transmitted through bad injection practices that causes chronic liver disease. The liver is the largest solid organ and the largest gland in the human body and it aides in filtering the blood from outside compounds like drugs and alcohol, it stores essential vitamins and minerals, it supports immune system activity and so much more. There's no question that the ramifications of living with a diseased liver are not only unhealthy but fatal. Sadly, she was subjecting every person she chose to share needles with to the same thing. I told you, the risks she took to get high were king size. Absolutely giant consequences. I'd be perfectly ok if I never saw another needle again.

Additionally, when you think about the side effects of addiction, you would never contemplate having a strong sense of independence as being one of them. It's a characteristic usually associated with self-motivators and overachievers. A good thing. Unless that independence comes as a direct result of not trusting people and the basis of it is more defensive in nature. In the most common sense, independence is achieved through the removal of someone or something that provided assistance; exemption from reliance. It's the ability to complete tasks independently or by oneself. For fact's sake, I could never rely on Rose for a single thing. She couldn't even rely on herself

164

most of the time. And because I couldn't trust her, I felt like I couldn't really trust anybody. Except daddy, of course. He always came through. He just doesn't count. So, I developed an "I don't care" attitude. I didn't develop a strong sense of independence as a byproduct of having made mistakes and learning to capitalize on them as an instinct to trust myself, essentially learning to stand on my own two feet. Or having been guided by someone and then gaining independent stability. It was birthed out of anger and disappointment. Not being able to trust your own mom is something straight out of the pits of dysfunctional hell. Remember this, "I'm staying clean this time. You don't have to worry about that", the famous line she gave me in the car after leaving the bus station. I wanted to trust the words that were coming out of her mouth, I wanted to think that she actually believed the words that she was saying. Though they sounded good, they were just that, words. She was yet to follow through on that promise and anything else she would say to me as a child to make herself feel better. She was quite skilled at persuading people through her perfected art of "fast talking" and because I had been duped so many times, my ears were like cups with holes in them, taking it all in as it was all falling right back out. I'm aware that Rose couldn't fully control her thoughts and emotions, and the worthless commentary she regurgitated was only designed to get her through the tough moments at hand. Saying whatever was required of her to proceed with life, with total disregard for what her words meant to the person receiving them. But at what point do you just remain silent, instead of repeating worthless rhetoric? It would have been better for her to just give me a break from the barrenness of her words.

I've always been taught that your word is your bond. It stamps a seal of approval on your integrity and character as a person. It solidifies that you are who you say you are, and you will do what you said you would. Traits that Rose would never seem to attain or value. In turn, I had severe trust issues with people. Questioning every motive about everything. As if there was some rocket science to believing people about genuinely wanting to do nice things for me or invite me to some place fun. Were they doing this to get a ton of spending money from daddy? Or for cool points so they could ask for something later down the road? Stupid indeed. But that was where my lack of trust and my inability to rely on Rose had left me with other people. Was it unfair? Absolutely. This would go on for a while, in adolescence and well into young adulthood. The corner store in the projects was nothing new to me. I had been there a hundred times over buying junk to fill up on. But just about every time I opened the metal burglar bar door to enter the store, I was accompanied by someone. My cousin, Tonya or another kid from the projects. I had never been to the store alone. It was creepy. Even with someone there it was still creepy. You could barely get inside because the door was usually blocked by drunk men standing outside drinking forty ounce beers from a brown paper bag. There were a decent number of guys in their late teens and early twenties wearing layers of gold chains and gold teeth standing around too. Clearly, they were on their drug posts. There were at least twenty or so people outside of the store at any given time. Around the age of twelve, my attitude would get the best of me and I would make the senseless decision to walk to the corner store by myself, after all, I didn't care right. It was pretty stupid and bona fide dangerous. I was subjecting myself to inappropriate cat calls of "Hey lil mama, let me holla at you", or "You don't need that candy, I can be your sugar daddy" from grown men. Gross! Or worse, the risk of being physically preyed upon. No tween girl should walk anywhere alone, especially not in the projects. A lot of stealing took place in that store, and people would often grab stuff and fly out the door in a vigorous getaway. What if a fight had broken out in one of those aisles like I had witnessed before or shots had been fired? Thank heaven none of those horrible things happened, but they were still potential possibilities. But I was satisfied with depending on me to get what I wanted in that moment. And I wanted nothing more than to walk to that store as an excuse to have the opportunity to spot Rose amongst the constant chaos. Though I had no plans to say a word to her, all I wanted to do was put my eyes on her to make sure she was still alive. I walked right into disappointment though, because she was nowhere to be seen. It was tremendously foolish, but to me it was a risk worth taking. Creepily similar to the risks she was taking by making the decision to shoot up, in the sense that the outcome outweighed the danger. There's a stark difference, though: the risk I took was out of love and concern for her well-being. Looking back, it was a risk I would probably never take again. Her risks were selfish, deadly and repetitive. That strong sense of independence and "I don't care attitude" made me naive to the menace of what walking alone actually subjected me to. That wasn't independence at all. It was control. Selfish indignation. I could try and create the results that I wanted since that wasn't the case with Rose, I couldn't get any qualifiable progress out of her. Nothing I did would alter her conclusions. But I could try and regulate my own world as much as possible. It definitely wasn't always successful, but it was how I operated. Taking over every situation as much as I could, even if it meant inviting hazards or pissing people off. In school and work situations, it was pushing people away because it made me appear bossy.

There's no doubt, I'm a take charge kind of girl, but bossy would mean that nobody had any input but me and I wasn't easy to work with since I couldn't be a team player. That perception wasn't going to work! I had to change that quickly. But there's no telling how many people I pushed away before I got my act together. It's explicitly impossible to substitute character traits and expect success. Let's be clear, side effects are usually characterized by an undesirable result of a drug or form of treatment, but for someone who has never even touched a cigarette with a ten foot pole, I was a surrogate for all of the instinctual symptoms of human awareness for both me and Rose. Carrying all of the psychological manifestations of "I have to stop living like this", "let me try something different" or "what must people think of me?" You know, those same emotional nudges that prompt us to stop having late night dessert after you have noticed a ten pound weight gain or to make a conscious decision to commit to working out three days a week. I was harboring additional side effects of Rose's lack of self-accountability. Ironically, I wasn't even the drug abuser, but I was experiencing more unwarranted consequences than she was.

You don't have to be sick to get better and inadvertently, you don't have to be a drug user to be sick either. Rose always seemed to be carrying the heaviest bricks life had to hand her, and without even asking for my help, she handed the load right to me. Usually, in most normal situations, just the opposite happens. Parents take on the burdens of their children and work feverishly to ease them. Pause for a second and contemplate this. **What do you do when you have to live with other people's choices?** Goodness gracious! The very implied reality of that is something so burdensome that it will make you bury your face into a pillow and scream. Yet, it was a daily truth for me. I became crippled by fear, compulsively worrisome and keenly socially aware. Metamorphosing into an assiduous student, laser focused on understanding the risks she was taking with needle

"What do you do when you have to live with other people's choices?"

sharing, and Hepatitis C almost seemed bearable because HIV and AIDS cases amongst blacks had monumental increases in the 1990's, and the likelihood that she would contract such an incurable disease was the heaviest brick of them all to carry. I can recall doing as many as four detailed school reports, proclaiming myself as an expert on the subject and mentally preparing for what I was assured was inevitable. That was fear.

And rather than catching up on the latest episodes of sitcom gold like *Martin* and *The Fresh Prince of Bel-Air*, I was completely infatuated with prison documentaries, where cameras would go behind bars in some of the country's toughest prisons and capture the real life experiences of what life as an inmate was like. Trying fiercely to catch a glimpse of what Rose was possibly living like while incarcerated. Prison seemed far more dangerous than even being on the streets, the tensions were astronomical as it was filled with some of the most violent people, fighting was a surety and inmates were skilled at making weapons out of everyday writing supplies like ink pens and paper clips. Some even managed to steal a knife from the kitchen for an even more dangerous weapon. Items like ramen noodles, gum and postage stamps that were purchased at the prison commissary were being stolen, and in many cases were landing inmates in solitary confinement for the vicious attacks they evoked as they tried to retrieve them. The prison infirmary was as overcrowded as a county hospital in Anywhere, USA. There was no way to escape the daily threats and fighting and hiding stuff became survival tactics. The most depressing thing to witness in all of it, were the pregnant women who found themselves living in those conditions and whose children were to be born in them as well. I couldn't help but see Rose as one of those women and myself as that unborn child. I managed to escape the extreme possibility of birth in such a horrific place, but the margin had to be razor thin. I was born in 1978 and in that year alone Rose had been arrested 18 times. Mostly for theft, but that's an average of 1.5 times per month. Almost twice a month, equates to about every two weeks. Think about that for a moment. She went to jail almost every two weeks for an entire year. It truly is a miracle I made it through the doors of the hospital. I'm so glad I didn't have to start life there. But those documentaries and the likelihood that Rose was living in those same conditions triggered my compulsive worrying.

My keen social awareness came from trying to decipher between the controversial argument the prison documentaries sparked, were they intended for rehabilitation or punishment? On some level, the treatment of the inmates seemed inhumane. We typically don't feel bad for people who find themselves locked behind bars, but prison conditions are regulated. And they are required to provide the bare necessities of cleanliness, food and adequate medical care. However, in many prisons across the country, basic human rights were being violated and prison reform efforts to quandary these issues were and still are, being stifled by the greed of only making money from the privatized prison system, instead of partaking in the real work of rehabilitating prisoners for credible re-acclimation back into society. I'm not necessarily a criminal sympathizer, as I firmly believe that actions have consequences and often those consequences will put you behind bars, but I don't see the value in just throwing people behind bars, many suffering from mental illness without the proper treatment and ability to acquire an education or trade to ensure their return is less likely. I am aware that drug treatment programs, GED classes and some trade classes are indeed available to inmates, but where is the emphasis on advocating that all prisoners take part in all of the programs like a checklist of prerequisites before even being considered for release? A system of checks and balances that certifies their growth. Only adapting increased survival skills like fighting to shield yourself from personal attacks is not conducive to finding employment on the outside. It's already overwhelming for a convicted felon to get a job, but doing so without any serious personal or educational gains seems catastrophic. And virtually impossible. Rose is a textbook example of the system failing. She never obtained her GED and though she had a few stints of sobriety and attended some drug rehabilitation classes, I am not persuaded that the coursework focused enough on her as an individual to try and get a greater understanding of what was causing her to retreat back to addiction. I'm sure this feat is impossible to attain for the entirety of the country's immense incarceration population without tremendous resources, but it just baffles me how the richest country in the world, with by far the highest incarceration rate in the world at more than five times higher than most every other country, has federal resources for less compelling things like, excessive travel for federal employees, tax cuts to the wealthiest of Americans and funding what is already the most powerful military in the world, but the bank is closed when it comes to being proactive about the well-being of one of its most marginalized groups of citizens. You decide, are prisons intended for rehabilitation or punishment? Or money? A combination of the latter two are at play for me. Unquestionably,

Rose put herself on the road that led to prison, just like she put herself on the same road that led to the alley and under the bridge. The same road that led her to eat cereal with tap water from the kitchen sink when my aunt didn't have milk because she was so parched for food, or find comfort in the bottom of a cheap bottle of wine that shared her name when she was in between hits, Wild Irish Rose. There was no substantive vice that she wouldn't touch. She paid for the steep price of drug addiction with her freedom, her sobriety, her health, her family and her social and economic prosperity. It just pains me that she was so deficient in getting the tools she needed and was left to navigate the world of addiction unequipped. Much like jumping out of a plane without a parachute, and watching her demise was no different than waiting for a heart monitor to flatline. Death was coming.

Now that you've chewed and washed down how Rose's choices caused me to be a fearful, worrisome person who was a socially aware needle hater with a "I don't care" attitude, I hope you are more premeditated about how your decisions impact other people, no matter how small. From the toothpaste we buy to the tires on our cars and what to make for dinner, there is almost no decision that we make that affects us alone. **Relationships are a lot like a business transaction. There should be an equal amount of exchange between the parties. But when we're forced to live with other people's choices, we don't get the luxury of weighing the assets versus the liabilities. Tolerably, we have to learn how to balance the books, pain versus compassion, not allowing ourselves to fall into a negative status. And far too often we pay double interest on some of those liabilities, enduring pain now and later down the road. The only way to build emotional wealth is to create a balanced portfolio of faith, prayer, patience, understanding and self-love. Make daily deposits through prayer. Pray, pray and pray some more, for strength and endurance. Allow yourself to feel the emotional weight of whatever circumstances the choices hand you and trust your intuition to handle them accordingly. Love yourself by setting boundaries on how much you can take and be discerning about the best way to walk away.**

These things are reasonable to do as an adult, but kids are not usually the decision makers in their own lives and their dealing will have to come with a healthy dose of help from others and a little creativity of their own making. If you stretch your arms out and place a multitude of bricks horizontally across them, you wouldn't have any problem holding them for a few seconds. But as time passes, those bricks get heavier and your arms undoubtedly get weaker, even for the strongest person. It's fair to note that I don't think Rose intentionally meant for me to carry her bricks, but she sure as hell didn't try to take them from me either. I don't think it really mattered who had to carry them, as long as she didn't. Carrying Rose's bricks everyday was unfair and unsolicited, my arms were much smaller than hers but turned out to be much stronger too.

Misfortune (noun) - an unfortunate condition or event.

"Fortune knocks but once, misfortune has much more patience." - Laurence J. Peter

Chapter 8
Misfortune

It had become a chronic occurrence for Rose to find herself handcuffed and sitting in the back of a police squad car, but in February 1990 at thirty-four years old, what seemed like a routine arrest would soon take a turn for the worst. Her addiction was at an all-time high and she became more accustomed to selling "bunk" drugs than just the one dreadful time I knew about to the known drug dealer who beat her. It was all such a sad recourse in an effort to keep her habit thriving. On one particular February afternoon, Rose could be identified by a Dallas Security Force officer as sitting on a porch in the projects, alone with a coat and a brown paper bag. She is said to have been moving the positioning of the bag from back and forth under her arm to between her knees. Making herself look

179

suspicious. Shortly after, another woman would approach Rose on the porch and demand she be given $10 back for having been sold some "bad dope". The confrontation would cause the officer to approach both of them in an attempt to diffuse the situation. Rose would continue to deny having done anything wrong as the other woman would also continue to demand her money back. The more intense the argument got, the larger the crowd of spectators would grow. Within minutes, several other officers would be on the scene to aide in the debacle. The other woman would go on to tell the officers that the jacket and brown bag on the porch belonged to Rose. One of the officers proceeded to pick up the bag and found inside two blue "dime baggies" and a crack pipe. Because no field tests were performed on site to verify that the substances in the blue baggies were actually crack cocaine, Rose was free to go until such tests could be performed.

Unfortunately, she was arrested a month later on a separate charge and wouldn't see life outside again for several years. With her being back in custody, the contents of the brown bag could then be tested and potentially held as evidence.

Forensics would prove the contents of the blue "dime baggies" to be a substitute for crack cocaine made of wax and soap shavings, the fake substance she had sold to the female addict demanding her money back, but the residue from the crack pipe would test positive for a controlled substance weighing in at 12 grams. Rose had just caught her first drug linked felony, not for an actual piece of crack, but albeit for the residue that remained in the crack pipe from a previous use. That would be the type of luck that Rose would have. At any given time, assuredly she would have had drugs in her possession, but the one day she actually didn't, she went down for the residue. Drugs are drugs, no matter the form or the amount, it just seemed like such unfortunate circumstances for somebody like her. She would be sentenced by a jury in October 1990 to 29 years of confinement in the Texas Department of Corrections.

See what I mean by everybody in the projects knew about Rose. Not only was she a known addict, but a "bunk" dealer too, and those confrontations would only continue to provide negative attention for her. This is why I constantly engaged in verbal wars, trying my best to defend the indefensible. A job I should have never had in the first place. In the month between the two arrests, Rose would return to business as usual. That meant participating in her daily habits of getting high. It's pretty stupefying that she hadn't been charged with a drug-related felony prior to the February episode. Just a short time before, Ms. Walker's apartment would be raided for incidents that involved flushing drugs down the toilet and for finding drug paraphernalia. Rose was living there at the time and was assumed to be involved, but because the apartment belonged to the senior citizen Ms. Walker, charges were only filed against her. Rose had just narrowly escaped being hit like a target at shooting practice. As a result, Ms. Walker would be evicted by the Dallas Housing Authority for smoking crack cocaine and for allowing her apartment to be used as a "dope house".

Ms. Walker, who appeared to be sweet, lonely and being taken advantage of, was not only enabling Rose, but was a crack smoking addict herself. Jesus! What in all of the earth would make a senior citizen in her situation smoke crack? I don't know exactly how old Ms. Walker was, but she had to be at least 65 to even be in the senior citizen section of the projects. What an incredibly devastating discovery. How long had she been smoking crack? Was she a recovering addict that relapsed? If so, how long had it been? Did Rose introduce it to her? Or had she been an addict all along? It was indeed a heinous revelation, as most chronic addicts don't live to see 65. This is why she perplexes me. I swear she had me fooled, and maybe the daily routine of sitting on the porch with her glass of lemonade was relevant to her lonely old lady portrayal, mirroring the same self-pity that Rose would normally inflict. I see, this self-pity concept was really offering big paybacks for them. And these two needed awards for their Oscar winning performances. Between the chatter about fried shrimp and the game show Wheel of Fortune, Mrs. Walker had deceived me. It makes sense now why Rose was so comfortable sitting at the table in Ms. Walker's kitchen freebasing. The obvious nature of their relationship would suggest that they must have sat there together a few times. As for the drug paraphernalia found by the cops, there's no doubt it belonged to both of them. By the time the February incident was playing out, Rose was back to living on the streets

183

and Mrs. Walker had found a permanent residence behind bars. But why would Rose purposely take me to that drug infested place? She was again deliberately putting me in harm's way. And for what? I couldn't serve as a prop that time.

The truth about Ms. Walker would be revealed at Rose's trial for felony possession of a controlled substance. Though Rose tried to appeal the conviction, the evidence would prove far too damaging and the sentencing would stand. Rose was a repeat offender and even the jury had a hard time trying to substantiate her plea of "not guilty." But one juror did find sympathy and classified her more as a person who had a severe addiction and not necessarily as a true criminal. The human element of compassion would come to life for one particular female juror while serving on Rose's case. The juror would pen a letter to Rose after the trial and it would read as such:

Dear Rosie,

As a member of the jury, I thought hard and long about your case. It has been a long and difficult process but very fair. As you leave the courtroom today, I want you to know that my prayers will turn to you often. I want you to know that I value you and believe that with God's help you can and will make a positive contribution to this world. All of us have made choices in our lives and done things that we wish we hadn't. The only thing I know to tell you is this, pick yourself up, brush the dirt off, and go on with your life. Make the best of every opportunity so that when I see you again, there is rejoicing over your victory over your past. I know you can do it. Don't let anyone tell you otherwise.

- Female Juror

Dear Rosie,

As a member of the jury, I thought hard and long about your case. It has been a long, difficult process, but very fair.

As you leave the courtroom today, I want you to know that my prayers will turn to you often. I want you to know that I value you and believe that with God's help, you can and will make a positive contribution to this world.

All of us have made choices in our lives that and done things that we wish we hadn't. The only thing I know to tell you is this: Pick yourself up, brush the dirt off, and go on with your life. Make the best of every opportunity so that when I see you again, there is rejoicing over your victory over your past. I know you can do it. Don't let anyone tell you otherwise.

Sincerely,

FILED
OCT 26 1990

Obviously, I wasn't the only one who appeared to pity Rose, perfect strangers did too. And once again, someone else seemed to care more about her future and sobriety than she actually did.

From January 1991 to April 1993 Rose served time in the state penitentiary for that felony conviction. After her release she would resort back to the same familiarities and would violate the terms of her parole and was right back in the penitentiary for a second time from August 1995 to May 2000. She never got any additional time, she just continued to get time served on the previously imposed 29 year sentence.

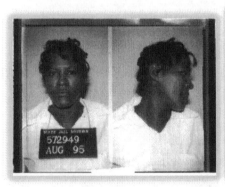

After almost six years in a medium security facility and drug free, I picked her up from that Greyhound bus station. And you know the rest, two weeks later she left the "mansion" and started her free fall to a mental Armageddon, the place where the final battle would be fought, in her mind between the psychological forces of good and evil. Honestly, this cycle was exhausting. As much as it was for me, it had to be even more so for her. There was no going back though, a new day had dawned as I had made up my mind that I was no longer going to be concerned with Rose's whereabouts. She was obviously doing what she wanted to do, and I was losing precious time with my own family. There was just no way to continue in this malignant and draining relationship without running the risk of totally losing myself. I couldn't afford to give her and her addiction that much power any longer. My heart, emotions and energy were utterly bankrupt. The lone juror who took interest in her future about nine years prior would have been gravely disappointed that nothing had penetrated deep enough to get Rose to change her harmful lifestyle. Sadly, nothing would.

Rose would make no major adjustments to her way of living and would frequently find herself behind bars every year, several times a year, for at least the next six years. She went to jail for everything from criminal trespassing to theft and numerous parole violations. She even found herself in the Texas Department of Corrections for a third time, but mostly just as an addict in drug rehabilitation classes from February 2006 to April 2006. At this point I'm sure she and all of the correctional officers were on a first name basis. It didn't seem like Rose was even trying to jump out of the revolving door that led in and out of jail and the penitentiary, somehow, she was taking extra trips.

And be that as it may...*I was done taking rides with her.*

**BASIC INFORMATION RELATING TO OFFENDER (INMATE)
OF TEXAS DEPARTMENT OF CRIMINAL JUSTICE**
Public Information Disclosure Sheet as stipulated by Section
552.029

Name: <u>Curlee, Rosie Lee</u>   Identification Number: <u>572949</u>

DOB: <u>07/20/1955</u>   Race/Gender: <u>B/F</u>

<u>Controlling Offense:</u>

Charge: <u>Poss. Cocaine Habitual</u>   Sentenced: <u>10/26/1991</u>

County/Court: <u>Dallas</u>

    Minimum Expiration of Sentence Date: <u>10/16/2005</u>

    Maximum Expiration of Sentence Date: <u>03/24/2021</u>

    Date received: <u>01/07/1991</u>

    Sentence began Date: <u>05/14/1990</u>

    Date Released: <u>04/13/1993(Parole, Ret'd 08/16/1995, Rel'd Parole 05/15/2000,
Ret'd 02/09/2006, Rel'd ISF 04/06/2006)</u>

    Date Discharged: <u>N/A</u>

<u>Additional Sentences:</u>

Charge: <u>Poss. Cocaine</u>   TDCJ: <u>572949</u>

County/Court: <u>Dallas</u>   Sentenced: <u>11/01/1991</u>

    Minimum Expiration of Sentence Date: <u>03/24/2000</u>

    Maximum Expiration of Sentence Date: <u>03/24/2000</u>

    Date received: <u>01/07/1991</u>

    Sentence began Date: <u>05/14/1990</u>

    Date Released: <u>04/13/1993(Parole, Ret'd 08/16/1995)</u>

    Date Discharged: <u>03/24/2000</u>

Angel Wings (noun) - angel wings are associated with the spiritual, a higher evolution of the soul, higher realms of existence or ascension.

"And then I heard the angel say, she's with you everyday." - unknown

"Those we LOVE don't go away, they walk beside us everyday, unseen, unheard but always near. Still loved, still missed and very dear." – unknown

CHAPTER 9
ANGEL WINGS

Undoubtedly the drug rehab classes weren't working, and Rose would keep repeating this death trap. In the end, her body just couldn't sustain any further damage from the poison. On June 10, 2006 at the young age of 50, Rose gained her wings. She lost her battle with addiction and succumbed to the power of drugs, just one month shy of her 51st birthday. The demons she could never overcome would win.

Death was always going to be the end result. It was only a question of when. And I remain indoctrinated that her frequent visits to jail are what allowed her to stay alive for as long as she did. I told you, only time would tell, and it never seemed to be on her side. It ultimately wasn't. I wish more than anything that I had more joyous memories with my mom. But precious remembrances from others tell the story of a woman who loved to sing, dance and play softball. I went to a slew of baseball games and engaged in the sport at school and summer camp, so it would have been comically amusing to see her try and catch

the pop fly balls I had come to be known for. I was a decent dancer, and I definitely couldn't sing, but you couldn't stop me from standing on the bathroom counter, singing into a hairbrush pretending to be a contestant on Star Search. I'm sure she could have showed me a thing or to, if nothing else it would have been a blast trying. Mom was obviously more than just an addict, but I missed out on seeing that side of her. I think that part had pretty much dissolved into oblivion by the time I was born. I just can't figure it out, but she was content with what she had allowed herself to be. If she wasn't, she would have put forth more effort into her sobriety. She had several legitimate shots at it. Just like a baby determined to learn how to walk, they keep falling but never give up until they have mastered the skill. Where was her fight? Her get back up? Her desire to live? It was almost like she was committing a slow suicide on purpose. And there's nothing more

tortuous and painful than watching someone you love, especially the one who gave you life, throw in the towel and voluntarily take their own. It all felt like cruel and unusual punishment. Mom never attempted to get a job, she ran away from halfway houses, she abruptly left the "mansion" and she was obviously not taking advantage of being in rehab. In being there she was only offering her physical presence; her mental presence wasn't anywhere in the room. I don't have a crystal ball, so I can only imagine that insecurity and doubt must have been metastasizing like a cancerous tumor in her head, since rehab was forecasting sobriety with a chance of relapse. How was she supposed to get good at staying clean when making the slightest mistake had a chance of killing her? She had to be poignantly gutsy, resolute and brave. All of that would take a scaffold for her to reach. I still believe that if the classes had focused more on her as an individual and sought to comprehend the depths of her addiction at its core, perhaps notable steps could have been achieved. Sadly, they didn't. She continued to reside in a constant crippling state of hopelessness, where drugs didn't judge her, they made her feel good and falsely took away her pain.

Mom may have been an addict, but she was still a human, with human emotions. When sober, she would write me letters often and express her regret for allowing herself to be in prison. Those emotions needed to be explored and dissected for truth and relevance by someone. She talked about a better day and encouraged me to continue excelling in school. And every letter would always include a hand drawn piece of art. It was a common practice for inmates. Winnie the Pooh and Mickey Mouse are the two that I remember most. I cherished those letters and stored them safely in my sock drawer. I just wish someone had cherished her healing in the same way. See, those delicate moments spent in prison where she could reflect on why she was there and the regret she finally showed, that had to have been the true essence of who she was. There's good in all of us, and her delayed contrition was proof that it was in there somewhere.

I don't think Rose wanted to be an addict, she settled for being one. Drugs were like that abusive partner that just wouldn't let her go. I've already made my claim that investing in serious resources and hiring more qualified individuals is one step towards repelling this enormous problem. I fully acknowledge that this is a pretty hefty undertaking that would require lawmakers to be purposeful about prison reform and its potential benefits and pass legislation that would make personalized help certain. It's as unlikely as ending mass incarceration altogether, especially when you consider the hard truth that private prisons are considered a business, and why invest in them to better society when everyone can get rich at the hands of free labor? I won't hold my breath, just like I didn't waiting for my mom to finally kick a habit that had bullied her for decades. But it sure would have been nice to see a genuine effort for a woman who appeared vulnerable enough to allow someone into her head. Instead, she was lumped into a group of all different kinds of addicts and was expected to allow generalizations about drug abuse and offers of "typical" coping mechanisms to infiltrate her already fragile mental and physical state. Like a one size fits all remedy. It was no different than putting doctors in a room and expecting all of them to perform open heart surgery, regardless of their varied levels of education and training or lack thereof. With the implied approach, here are the tools you need, now let's get busy.

Or maybe even centralized attention wouldn't have been enough. I can't say for certain, but it would definitely have been a start. Rose had to be invested in her own success. Very calculated about her next move. And it just never seemed to exist. Just as shame and self-disgust most often didn't. I can't fully account for what Rose was living with, but if I were a gambling woman, I would place a high stake Las Vegas style bet on the fact that she was probably masking another form of mental illness with her addiction as well, which was greatly magnified due to the drugs and because she wasn't properly served, no attempts at "regular" treatment would be adequate. She needed localized, concentrated help, the kind of help she would never receive. The kind of help that a prison in its current state can't sufficiently provide, especially when you inhale the grimacing fact that in the state of Texas, the county jail is the leading mental health provider.

Then there's the possibility that I'm completely wrong about need focused attention. Rose appeared to have enough strength and know-how for the things that mattered to her, she was a mastermind at pulling things off for her purposes. She managed to reinvent "bunk" drugs out of soap and wax, she found a van to use to steal from stores, she could inflict self-pity on people in a nanosecond to get what she needed, and she was persuasive in giving the appearance of a model prisoner to aide in her release. Her psychological functions were perfectly intact when she drafted a blueprint of those plans. But why couldn't she put that much effort into her own success? What was the purpose of using so much energy for her own demise? The only thing that comes to mind is this: Rose didn't love herself and because she didn't, she was incapable of loving me. I mean that in the gentlest maternal way possible. Her normal motherly instincts and emotions had been hijacked by the drugs that would ultimately alter her brain function. Knowing this, I'm still not able to squarely plant my feet on "she didn't know any better". She was a highly functioning person and there are those who have far more severe brain abnormalities than she that know right from wrong. I had unconditional love for her though and in spite of everything, I would never let that little spark of hope die.

The day Rose died was all so tragic too. There was not a single event that involved her in which any series of steps appeared to make sense. Her misfortunes were too numerous to count, even in death. I was shopping at the mall with my kids when my phone rang. Hesitant to answer because I didn't recognize the number. It was a family member telling me to rush to the hospital because my mom was in cardiac arrest and the doctors were having a hard time resuscitating her. I grabbed the kids from the stationary play area and rushed to the parking garage. While impatiently waiting for the elevator, I called daddy and repeated what I had just been told. In typical daddy style, he asked no questions and hurried to meet me and the kids at the hospital. When I arrived, a nurse seated us in the waiting room and I waited for daddy. Even though my phone had rung with the news, not a single family member was there. What a calamitous reality. Whether Rose had depleted all of her sympathy or not with them, or how tired they were of dealing with her antics, the mere fact that the doctors were having trouble resuscitating her was indicative that death was a certainty. Tragically, that wasn't enough to move anybody's feet. It was indisputable that they considered her solely my responsibility. I'll be the first to admit, Rose should have booked herself on an apology tour decades before, but that's no excuse for the absence of damn near everyone. Especially in the face of death. She died at the hospital alone. Daddy got there just in time to sit with the kids while the same nurse escorted me back to identify the body. We walked down a short hall and across the nurse's station to a room at the end of the hall.

Before walking into the room, the nurse paused, and asked, "Are you ready?" Of course, I wasn't ready, but what options did I have in that moment? I couldn't control this outcome. She opened the door and I slowly followed behind her. It was very dim, I could barely see, and the temperature was so cold that I started to shiver. She walked to the top of the bed and slightly pulled back the white sheet so I could see the full face. "Is this your mom?" she asked. A slow nod and a weak "yes" would follow. There she lay, with that beautiful dark ebony skin, and a head full of gray. The feeling of overwhelming loss and sadness did not consume me, only pity, sorrow and soul freeing relief did. Why did her life have to come to this? But finally, at long last, she was free. Totally free. Free from jail. Free from addiction. Free from mental bondage and hopelessness. "Rest in peace mama. Rest in eternal peace." No sooner than those words could leave my mouth in graciously anguished and repetitious fashion, I could feel the nurse gently touch my shoulder to offer comfort. A clear sign that God was telling me, that even in this moment of affliction He would be there.

The doctor who had been treating her would stop me on my way back to the waiting room to inform me that she had suffered a heart attack and couldn't be revived after going into cardiac arrest. Her heart was just too weak. After 30 years of drug use, a considerable amount of fluid had built up around her heart, causing pressure. This was the second time, as she had battled through a heart attack once before. Add to that the truly chilling day that she jousted with the side effects of having smoked some "bad dope" and lay powerless in an emergency room bed, clutching at her heart with paralyzing chest discomfort. Selfishly seeking the medical team's assistance in taking away the pain that she and her crack pipe blissfully invited. Pain that she could only explicitly describe as "It feels like my chest is caving in." She was searching for a high, but ended up staring down the barrel of her own mortality. This ridiculous rationale that there are "good" and "bad" versions of dope is detestable and hands down one of the dumbest things I've ever heard. As if using "good dope" is somehow better and you live to tell about it. The doctor went on to say that a urine sample would confirm a positive test for cocaine and a blood test would reveal sepsis, a blood infection. Even with a weak heart, Diabetes and Hepatitis C, and the likelihood that death was imminent, Rose still chose to grab cocaine, her abusive life partner by the hand, pull it close, hug it tight and kiss it on the cheek one last time. Affectionately showing her love for what didn't love her back. And it was indeed her last time. A few days later, daddy, my hubby and I would meet at the funeral home to plan a small home-going celebration. As we went about the business of picking out caskets and deciding on a final resting place, I sat in total adoration of daddy. Taking my best shot at holding back tears. I didn't have tears for Rose, but I did have happy ones for the father she had given me. He and mom hadn't been together in over 20 years at that point, but he was the first person to show up to the hospital and the only person who would help me carry this huge financial load. There's no greater man than him. He is an angel with a human face.

But who didn't see this coming? Here we both were, taking care of the steep price tag that was being dumped into our laps for the proper burial of the woman who didn't seem to care enough about or value either one of us. And we wouldn't have it any other way. She had given daddy and me both a gift, each other. I left there with my heart full and on assignment to write some nice departing words for

SUNRISE
July 20, 1955

SUNSET
June 10, 2006

*The Home-going Celebration
for the Life of*
Rosie Lee Curlee

SERVICE
SATURDAY, JUNE 17, 2006
11:00 A.M.

EVERGREEN MEMORIAL CHAPEL
6449 S. Houston School Rd • Dallas, TX

Allen Gene Madison, II
OFFICIATING

Rose's obituary. This task felt gargantuan. Obituaries were life resumes that entailed all of a person's accomplishments and were filled with meaningful words of expression. What was the kid who had been intentionally taken to a dope house and used as a prop for theft supposed to say? There was literally nothing to write about. I struggled greatly with emotional connectivity to Rose before she passed, and her sudden death hadn't caused me to make any drastic strides. The words I would come to formulate were very blunt in context and spoke directly to her steadfast and incessant demeanor towards drugs. Frankly, it was like trying to rationalize taking a knife made of drugs, stabbing it my heart, then wrapping a bow around it. They weren't heartfelt sentiments of gratitude and loss but rather of sensitivity and my hopes for her that never came to pass while she was still on this earth. They read:

To Our Mother,

It has been our desire that your soul find rest, that your heart find love and that your spirit find peace. Now that you have found the perfect resting place, all of our wishes for you have been fulfilled, and that makes our hearts smile. We knew you as a woman of strong will, persistence and determination, and for that we are thankful. You loved us more than words could ever say, and for that we are thankful. You taught us the true meaning of unconditional love, and for that we are thankful. You were a fighter, a survivor and one of the strongest people we knew, but fight no more and let your soul find rest until we meet again.   - Your Daughters

I wish I had more decorous things to say about her. More proud moments to share. I knew so little about her as a person that I couldn't even tell you her favorite color. I spent the majority of my young life wondering what it would be like to meet the parent I had never met. I just didn't have the pleasure of meeting my mom, only the ghostlike imposter who paraded around in her body as a helpless addict we called Rose. And consequently, there was always a part of me missing. A couple of days later, we buried Rose in that same lavender dress she had worn to my wedding. I sat on the front row during the ceremony and when it came time to say our final goodbyes, I stood hand and hand with daddy over the casket and he whispered, "Say goodbye to your mama." I did as he requested and let out a sorrowful, "Bye mama." But my mom was gone long before that day, and daddy didn't know that I had already said my goodbyes. I said them just about every time I saw her, not knowing if that would be my last, and again in that cold, dark hospital room. I was so broken, but I loved this woman in spite of all the pain. Love was the drug that we both needed and the one our hearts would never get enough of.

1891-06-JM

AMENDMENT TO MEDICAL CERTIFICATION OF CERTIFICATE OF DEATH

STATE OF TEXAS

STATE FILE NUMBER

ENTER NAME OF DECEASED AND PLACE OF DEATH EXACTLY AS SHOWN ON ORIGINAL DEATH CERTIFICATE

NAME OF DECEASED: Rosie Lee Curlee

DATE OF DEATH: June 10, 2006

PLACE OF DEATH (City or Town and County): Dallas, Dallas County, Texas

IS THE DATE OF DEATH BEING CORRECTED? ☐ Yes ☒ No

26. CERTIFIER (Check only one):
☐ Certifying Physician
☒ Medical Examiner/Justice of the Peace

27. SIGNATURE OF CERTIFIER

28. DATE CERTIFIED: 07/31/2006

29. LICENSE NUMBER: J1728

30. TIME OF DEATH: 2:37 P.M.

31. PRINTED NAME, ADDRESS OF CERTIFIER: Joni L. McClain, M.D. 5230 Medical Center Dr Dallas, Texas 75235

32. TITLE OF CERTIFIER: Medical Examiner

33. PART 1.
a. Sepsis due to a urinary tract infection associated
b. with diabetes mellitus
c.
d.

Approximate interval Onset to death: Unknown

PART 2. Hepatitis C; History of cocaine usage

34. WAS AN AUTOPSY PERFORMED? ☐ Yes ☒ No

35. WERE AUTOPSY FINDINGS AVAILABLE TO COMPLETE THE CAUSE OF DEATH? ☐ Yes ☒ No

36. MANNER OF DEATH: ☒ Natural ☐ Accident ☐ Suicide ☐ Homicide ☐ Pending Investigation ☐ Could Not Be Determined

37. DID TOBACCO CONTRIBUTE TO DEATH? ☐ Yes ☐ No ☐ Probably ☒ Unknown

38. IF FEMALE: ☒ Unknown if pregnant within the past year

42a. REGISTRAR FILE NO.: 02-04575

42b. DATE RECEIVED BY LOCAL REGISTRAR: August 08, 2006

42c. SIGNATURE OF LOCAL REGISTRAR

VS-174 REV 1/2006

"Godsent" (adjective) **-** an unexpected thing, event or person that is particularly welcomed and timely, as if **sent** by **God**.

"When someone comes into your life, God sent them for a reason. Either to learn from them or be with them till the end."
– unknown

CHAPTER 10
GODSENT MOTHERS

Tragedy has a way of awakening our inner strength. Bringing forth our human inclination to either fight or flight. There's no question about it, I was born a fighter. But even the strongest soldiers need help sometimes. My help came from several women, each of whom possessed their own set of superpowers. In each period of my life there was always another woman willing to fill in the gaps for Rose. My dad's sister taught me all about makeup and clothes and would let me destroy her closet trying on every piece of sequin clothing and high heels I could find. I'd paint my lips with ruby red lipstick and strut down the hallway with a boa and long sleeve gloves, mimicking the beautiful ladies of the Harlem Renaissance. Then in a flash, I'd come back out with my ice-skating leotard on and leg warmers, giving my best impression of Debbie Allen in *Fame*. I would go on for hours turning myself into new characters. My aunt would sit on the couch and just laugh. She would even give me ideas on who to be

next. But man, I sure made a mess. Clothes were sprinkled all over the place, from the bedroom to the kitchen. And I would have to solicit her help to clean it all up. She was so cool about it and this would become routine entertainment every time I stayed at my aunt's house. Mom never crossed my mind on those days, and it felt great to just be a kid.

Then there was my godmother. The Arkansas native with an extensive educational and professional background in social work and family therapy. She was an incredibly bright woman with such a gentle and loving spirit. She and my dad had become friends at work, and it didn't take a genius to see why

daddy thought she would be a phenomenal resource for love and

support. She was a devout

Christian and church

goer, and much of what I

learned about Christ came

from her dragging me to

church every weekend

and to vacation bible

school every summer. I'd

be lying if I said I was enthusiastic about having to stop playing

outside to go to Easter service rehearsals. But me and every

black kid I knew who was a part of a predominantly black

church was reciting a speech on Easter Sunday morning. As

much as I pitched a fit about going, I have to admit that I was

getting pretty good at the rapid fire game of reciting the books

of the bible. I never won that game, but we got some pretty good

belly laughs at each other as we struggled to pronounce

Deuteronomy, Ecclesiastes and Habakkuk really fast. I dare you

to try it. She and my godsister were big *Star Trek* fans and they would watch faithfully every week. They tried to get me to join them in that loyal event, but I am not a fan of sci-fi and back then I'd rather read an entire old school encyclopedia than watch it. But they had a great time together doing it. They even made popcorn and grabbed blankets to lay on the living floor as part of their customs. It was incredible to see them bonding as mother and daughter over an interest they both shared, and their satisfaction could be heard from every room in the house. Those moments made me emotional. Not because they had not persistently tried to include me, trust me, they did. But because I would never have those experiences with my own mom. Besides, I really hated *Star Trek*.

My godmother was always checking on me. She would pull me to the side on many occasions to ask how I was feeling and how she could help. She was easy to talk to and some days I engaged like an anxious kindergartner ranting all about the school day. Other times I just didn't feel like sharing and would give her a brief, "I'm ok", so I could get back to playing. When I did partake in expressing my feelings, she was gifted at putting things in relative terms so I could understand. Like the time she equated mom's condition to that of a sick patient in need of a team of doctors to get better. I was abreast of what she was trying to do, and I could envision being sick and needing help. That would explain her appearance, but Rose's actions were telling a different story.

My godmother was a beast in the kitchen too! We would often wake to the smell of bacon frying, scrambled eggs, warm pop tarts and orange slices for breakfast. On the weekends I spent the night, that was our Sunday and Monday morning breakfast. It was a simple feast, but it was so good. Maybe it was all the love it was prepared with, because the smell of bacon frying wasn't the only thing we awoke too, but the soulfulness of gospel music would be playing loudly, and we could hear her singing along as she danced around the kitchen cracking eggshells. She would kiss each of us on the forehead as we entered the kitchen to eat. She filled her home with the presence of God and in turn she filled me too. At that time in my life, Lord knows I needed a place of refuge from the projects and there was no better place than her home. There was always a whole lot of pure absurdity going on, but God always gave me what I needed and at precisely the right time. His timing was impeccable.

And just when I thought he had already given me his best; he sent my Mother-in-Love. I call her that on purpose. Actually, I only refer to her as mama. I met her when I was just 18 years old, and the last thing I was looking for was another mother. We started out on pretty shaky ground at first. I was coming into their lives at a time when her only son was on the road to fulfilling his youthful dream of being a professional athlete. I'm sure she was trying to gage me, looking to get a real temperature for the purpose I served in her son's life. He was a thriving 22 year old young man and he had never brought a girl home to meet his family. Let's face it, she probably wanted to know if I was a gold digger or if I was looking for a payout. The whole situation was awkward for all of us. But she would soon realize that me and her son had something special and I could care less about him playing football. I didn't need or want his money, my daddy had that covered and I had been going to professional football games for over a decade by the time he and I met. So, his playing football didn't really impress me. After we

Dope Girl   **Kimberly D. Mathis**

got through the testing phase of our new relationship, I discovered how easy she was to talk to. And I stayed in wonderment at her mean cooking skills. When we first met, she and her husband were living in Kansas City. Though lifelong Texans, they had moved there for work. When she came to visit us in Texas, she would make a fanciful spread so big that it would put any soul food restaurant to shame. Grandma had taught me a few things

along the way, but I wanted to learn how to cook like her. There was a stigma attached to a black girl from the South who couldn't throw down in the kitchen. I asked her more questions than a kid trying to figure out where babies came from and I was slowly compiling all of her recipes. She didn't hold back either, she shared everything with me and even started emailing them. This was indeed a good thing, because there are lots of family cooks who refuse to give up the ingredients to their beloved dishes. She was also an avid perfume collector, I'm sure this came from her time as a fragrance expert from a previous job, but her collection was boundless. I had never seen that much perfume, she had an entire department store full of it under the bathroom sink. There was nothing but various bottles on both sides. We would sit on the floor for hours smelling every one and rearranging the bottles in a pathetic attempt to clean it out. We were doing more sampling than we were cleaning, and I walked away with a vast new collection of my own. It was fun, because pleasant future in-law relationships were hard to come by. We got to the point where we called each other every day, talking about everything from how heavy the traffic was to the sales price of ground meat in the grocery store ad. The conversations weren't about much of anything, but it was fulfilling to have a mother figure to talk to. I talked to her more than my hubby did, I still do, and when we go out, if people ask us if she's my mom, the response is always a quick and definitive "yes." There's no need to correct them by saying, "Well actually she's my mother-in-law." She's just mama, plain and simple. By the time we started to have kids, she was an even greater tree of knowledge, and I had to call somebody to help me figure out how to deal with colic, teething and potty training.

It's crystal clear that everything I thought I had lost was being restored and I could no longer focus on what I didn't have but be exponentially grateful for what I did. Life has a way of taking you the long way around, but in more cases than not, we eventually get to where we're supposed to be. As my Mother-in-Love would say, "You've never seen a road that didn't bend." This reminds me of the famous quote by Theodore Parker, a minister of the Unitarian church whose words would go on to inspire a speech by Dr. Martin Luther King and would later be popularized by Barack Obama, "The arc of the moral universe is long, but it bends towards justice." I think Parker was referring to the moral degradation of slavery, and how befitting, because the mental captivity that Rose's addiction had caused me felt like slavery. And finding someone like mama was the justice I deserved.

My circle is impossible to complete without the spiritual and entrepreneurial mentorship of my pastor. This five foot-two inch beauty walked into my life wearing stilettos and sporting

215

blonde spiky hair. Her appearance was not that of a typical pastor. She was absolutely gorgeous and looked like she had just

walked right out of the pages of a fashion magazine. She had a stage presence that commanded your attention. She was small but ministered with such passion that her entire soul shined through. I had no intentions on getting to know her outside of just being pastor and the First Lady of the church, but because of the mutual relationships we shared, I found myself in her presence a lot. This woman was indeed intriguing. There was definitely a distinct chemistry between us, and it was not that of a casual pastoral relationship but more of a mother and daughter. It didn't take us long to start exchanging daily phone calls, sharing lunch dates and discussing ideas about how I could help her in the ministry. I found myself sitting on different committees for her upcoming women's conference and helping in the church nursery and bookstore. As much as she thought I was helping her, she was really the one helping me. The more I learned about her, the more I loved what she represented. And the more I would try to follow her example of excellence and selflessness. She was a smart college educated woman who gave up her lucrative career to go into full time ministry and be a stay-at-home mom. She was running the daily intricacies of the church and dealing with the lives of hundreds of women she was pastoring. Taking

on uncountable problems daily. Yet, she always found the time to lend me her ear or hold my hand and pray. At this point I had stopped worrying about Rose to the extent to which it consumed me, and I hadn't talked about her to anyone in quite some time. I don't know what prompted me to tell pastor about Rose and I was very vague without going into too much detail. But just the little I shared made her eyes swell as she grabbed both of my hands and said, "It's ok, daughter." And right on cue, a river of tears started to flow. She called me "daughter" and the term wasn't being used in the same breath as asking me for drug money. In a stroke of irony, my daughter would be born on pastor's birthday, sealing our forever bond. We were both short and fair skinned, and every place we went people just assumed that she was my birth mom. The look of astonishment on their faces when we would reveal we had no blood relation was something for the cameras to capture. We may not share blood, but we share the same spirit, love for our family and love for God. As I walked beside her, I learned how to balance being a mother and wife and how to still progressively pursue my own interests. I didn't have to navigate that world on my own like Rose did with addiction. And everything she poured into me I still stand on to this day. From *The Power of Prayer* to *The Power of Passion* and *Suffering in Silence*, her teachings and published literary works have given me immeasurable strength and there's just no way to fully express my gratitude. The distance between me and Rose would never be closed, and I just wasn't able to get what I desired out of her, but God saw fit to give me all the mothering I would ever need. Every last one of those women had an impact greater than they will ever understand. I carry a piece of each one of them with me every day. They were preparing me to be the mother that I would eventually become. Because of my aunt, my daughter had many days of childhood purity playing dress up, and I often turn into my godmother blasting gospel music in the kitchen. I have a collection of my Mother-in-Love's recipes to pass down and because of my pastor, my daughter will fully comprehend the power of prayer and life balance. When I look back over what God allowed me to endure, I can see His hand protecting and guiding me all along the way. And I recognize that some of the things that I underestimated would be the very things that would have the most value. They were lessons that I didn't even know that I was learning. Without question, I had the very best teachers.

My mom wasn't suited to teach me what they did, but she did teach me the meaning of unconditional love and what it feels like to forgive the unforgivable. You may never get an apology from someone who hurt you or let you down, stop looking for it. Forgive them anyway, even if they're not sorry. People can't give you emotionally what they don't possess. But you can make a deliberate decision to do what's best for you and release the pain. Just let it go. Healing is a choice. You have to consciously decide that you want to be free. Rose did apologize to me, but it felt empty and too late. Bitterness and anger had become my closest allies. But when I finally let go and stopped allowing myself to be a slave to the proverbial mental prison that her addiction had caused me, my soul exhaled one hell of a long breath. It's true, forgiveness is more for you than for them. And in case you haven't heard this before, un-forgiveness is like drinking poison and expecting the other person to die. Meanwhile, killing yourself. You've had to drink enough toxic potions from the heartache and weight of someone else's choices, be not intentional on mixing up your own cocktail.

Know this, nobody survives trauma without scars, but embrace them as the combat wounds that lead to your inner peace. Stop expecting yourself to have all the answers. Relax and trust the mending process. Understanding that every experience you encounter is carefully crafted to make you a mighty, tireless soldier and prove that you are battle tested. Embracing life's challenges as the faith strengthening, confidence building, character revealing and patience enduring tests that they are. It's a fact, what doesn't kill you makes you stronger, unequivocally. The more we learn to trust God and ourselves, the closer we get to living the life that we want and deserve. But decide to do it with a remorseless tenacity. Gaining assurance is a bonus gift that comes with freedom and healing, and self-confidence coupled with inner-strength are simply the most stylish clothes you can wear every day.

Gratefully, my kids are freed from the bondage of addiction, from verbal wars, impoverished mediocrity and jailhouse visits. There are no bridges to walk under, no alleys to pass and no creepy bus stations. More importantly, there are countless, faceless people just like Rose living in the hell of addiction and numerous other battles that life has made them fight. And there are that many more that are just like me. Trying our damndest to heal from things we couldn't discuss. But there is good news. There is no pain that God can't heal. No problem He can't solve. No burden He can't bear. Your life is not over!

It is not too late to live your truth. No matter what it is. Truth is the only safe ground to stand upon. You didn't come this far and pay this high of a price for nothing. God will meet you at the crossroads. Help is on the cusp of your praying lips, palmed hands, bent knees and bowed head.

What is God trying to heal you from?

I encourage you to find the strength to shed the shame of circumstances you can't or couldn't control. Let go of guilt, pain and the feeling of insufferable defeat. There is freedom and healing with your name on it. Forgive. And pray often, so tomorrow won't be like yesterday. God favors you and He favored me, and because He did, this girl turned out to be pretty dope.

Now, it's your turn. Be DOPE!

EPILOGUE
INSPIRED BY T. JACKSON

The relationship between me and Rose would not be one that would end as a nicely framed portrait. There would be no time stamping and cherishing its lasting beauty. Rather, it would end with lots of questions that would go unanswered. Questions of, who was she really? And what kind of mom would she have been? Both as a sober person of course. When Rose died my kids were the innocent ages of 4, 2 and 8 months old. I can count on a single hand how many times she had ever seen them. At such young ages, they would be handed their first trauma and would have to swallow the sourness of having to grow up without their grandma. I would be left to answer relentless questions of "Mom, where's your mom?" from a sweet 4-year-old, and my response of "She's in heaven with Jesus", just wouldn't be enough to satisfy her curiosities. Then, the hardest question of them all would come tenderly out of her mouth, "But, why is she with Jesus?" Before I could think of anything clever to say, she would abruptly finish her cross examination with, "Well, when can we go to heaven to see her?" Oh, baby girl, if we could, we would go every day with an arm full of roses just for Rose. I don't care how tough you are, no amount of mental fortitude can truly prepare you for the laborious chore of having to explain death to a child.

Though explaining to a child, the irrefutable nature of death is as gut wrenching and excruciating of an experience as any of us ever want to partake in, the throbbing pain of such an unwanted task and the concrete facts that result from it eventually diminish. Children are creatures of admirable resilience, and they are crafty at managing their emotions and containing any feelings of frustration, disappointment or anger. They bounce back from tragedy better than most adults and with great poise too. But that doesn't mean that throughout the process of growth and maturation, the residual effects of their experiences don't rear their ugly head through nefarious and rebellious activity. Our familial structure and environment are critical factors in how we manage pain. For me, I compartmentalized Rose's addiction into a skipping game pass the bridge and alley, dressing up and pretending to be the attorney that saved her, praying and embracing my catholic school rituals of making the sign of the cross, since in my head that gesture had magic powers, and at the height of my frustration, resorting to very explicit verbal exchanges and disregarding my own safety by probing the streets of the projects alone. But everyone processes pain in their own way and coping mechanisms are exclusive to each individual.

Let's take Tasha for example. A college junior working towards a degree in communications who splits her time outside of class on her campus job as a parks and recreation assistant, a dedicated member of her sorority and a sibling to three biological sisters and five other adoptive siblings. As a child, she and her biological sisters found themselves in one disastrous situation after another, as they were the product of a young, confused mother who had four children by the time she was 19. Tasha's mom Brenda and Rose's stories are eerily similar, and both involve them abandoning their parental responsibilities to their children and subjecting them to things that were unimaginable, since both were teenage moms who delved into drugs and prostitution very young. At seven years old, Tasha vividly recounts living in a run down, raggedy old duplex in a drug ravaged area of South Dallas, where she and her sisters lacked food and supervision as their mom frequently left them alone to immerse in her daily custom of both selling and using drugs. Sound familiar? They regularly missed school and "rocks"

225

of crack cocaine were always visible on the living room coffee table were the girls spent most of their time. Just sitting there in plain view. As Tasha grew older, she would repetitively hear, "You look just like your mama", as the similarities in their faces were undeniable. Since Tasha was not proud of what her mom had become and what she was starting to look like, her defiant behavior began. She tried desperately to change her appearance so she wouldn't be compared to her mom and took her first drastic step by dying her hair platinum blonde. That didn't work and the implied opinion would continue to be repeated, "You look just like your mama." Tasha took extreme measures and this time dyed one side of her hair a bright red and completely shaved the other. Nothing would free her from the shame she felt from people comparing them. And nothing short of plastic surgery actually would. "I don't look like her!" was her irate response since she could no longer identify her mom's beautiful face, only Brenda the addict was staring gravely back at her. But I can surely relate to how her pain was manifesting itself in her attitude.

Like me, Tasha can attribute her current success to the rigid matters of what her mom was subjecting her to and her greedy inclination NOT to live so gloomily. Instead, she further distanced herself from her mom's frightening truth by creating successes of her own. Tasha also had her adoptive parents to thank as they saved her and one of her birth sisters from the horror of seeing their mom busted by an undercover cop and their ill-advised choice to go visit her in an empty, drug saturated hotel room that she shared with strangers they didn't even know, all alone. Just two girls fiercely wanting to see if their mom was still alive, recklessly took measures that put themselves in danger to fulfill their worrisome instincts. I've been there. Done that. Thanks to my dad and Tasha's adoptive parents, we both managed to escape the never-ending list of terrible things that could have had life altering impacts on our success and who we were as people. However, kids of addicts in less structural atmospheres with far less adult impartation overwhelmingly turn to much more destructive behaviors. I don't know a more important human emotion than love, and addict kids crave love from their parents about as badly as the parents crave getting high, and commonly relate their relevance in their parents lives as insignificant since the parents seem to love drugs more than them.

Birthed from those feelings of not being loved comes the action of "finding love in all the wrong places". Sorrowfully, many teenage girls find themselves looking for love in the arms of men, some drastically older and freely participate in careless promiscuous behavior as an emotion filling band-aid. Usually already battling low self-esteem, this road typically leads to teenage pregnancy, only multiplying the pressures they were trying to flee from by essentially recreating the exact teenage mom pattern their moms had become and charged with giving their kids the love they never received. That's dysfunction at its finest. Others look for familial love and camaraderie in gangs, and we're all familiar with how violent, deadly and jail binding that life is. The most devastating coping mechanism is when the kids themselves turn to drugs, trying to escape the pain and feelings of unbearable rejection and sadness, becoming the same people they resented their parents for being. And the generational cycle of addiction continues. Most kids who find themselves caught in the web of addiction are motherless, fatherless or both. Left to weave through emotional turmoil, feelings of inadequacy, confusion, anger, bitterness and a host of other emotions. There's no doubt that being the child of an addict requires herculean strength and unless others genuinely intervene, the results are simply heartbreaking. We are all the culmination of everything we've been through, witnessed or experienced. And we may never understand why we have to endure the things we do to get to a particular place in life, but God willing, we come out on the other side, better and stronger.

Unfortunately, Rose did not have a happy ending and would not come out better on the other side, she would never get to stand on the bridge of triumph, but her score would be settled, and her victory would come through me. I have a marshmallow-like soft spot for families battling with addiction and often find myself encouraging and volunteering to help kids just like me and Tasha. Kids that find themselves in undeserving circumstances as a result of someone else's choices. I spent hours loving on six-year-old Brooklyn, who spent her nights in a homeless shelter and got dressed for kindergarten from boxes of donated clothes in the shelter's basement. Then there were those that were residents of the East Dallas housing projects and recipients of pre-packaged boxes of food that my NFL sisters and I had packed, designed to ease the burden of meals that would now be lost since school was out for the summer. I had spent my fair share of days as a project kid and I knew just how crucial those food boxes were. But nothing pulled at my heartstrings like watching the faces of poor mothers and their children light up as we informed them that they were the beneficiaries of a $1000-dollar shopping spree at Sam's Club. With pure joy we walked down the aisles beside them, pushing the shopping cart and watching them fill it with toys, clothes, TV's and everything in between.

Rose didn't give me what I needed, but I have made it my life's mission to volunteer and give back every chance I get. And just like I did as a kid, I transformed the burdens of those families into something I could manage, and in my heart and mind, my service was then and always is now, in Rose's honor. I guess things do have to fall apart so better things can come together.

Mama Can You Hear Me
By: Kimberly D. Mathis

Mama can you hear me,
I'm the growing baby in your womb.
Please stop feeding me poison, it makes me sick and leads us both to
doom.

Mama can you hear me,
I'm five years old today.
Headed to school with daddy,
passing you on the streets along the way.

Mama can you hear me,
You don't even look the same.
I'm in high school now and thriving,
but you still playing this deadly game.

Mama can you hear me,
I didn't sign up for this ride.
I love you, don't you miss me,
it's time for you to decide.

Mama can you hear me,
I'm screaming as loud as I can.
If you put down the pipe and needle,
I promise to hold your hand.

Mama can you hear me,
Why didn't you listen to what I said?
You loved something that didn't love you back,
now a casket covers your head.

Mama can you hear me,
I'm sending love to the sky.
You are now standing with Jesus,
I no longer have to cry.